PUB W
IN
County Durham

Other areas covered in the Pub Walks series include:

Bedfordshire
Berkshire
Birmingham & Coventry
Bournemouth & Poole
Bristol & Bath
Buckinghamshire
Cambridgeshire
Cheshire
Chilterns
Cotswolds
Cotswold Way
North & West Cumbria
South Cumbria
Dartmoor & South Devon
Derbyshire
Essex
West Essex
Exmoor & North Devon
Gloucestershire
Herefordshire
Hertfordshire
Icknield Way Path
Isle of Wight
Kent – the North Downs
Lancashire
Leicestershire & Rutland

Lincolnshire
North London
Middlesex & West London
Midshires Way
Norfolk
Northamptonshire
Nottinghamshire
Oxfordshire
Shropshire
South Downs
Staffordshire
Suffolk
Surrey
Surrey Hills
Thames Valley
North Wales
South Wales
Warwickshire
Wayfarer's Walk
Wiltshire
Worcestershire
Wye Valley & Forest of Dean
East Yorkshire
North Yorkshire
South Yorkshire
West Yorkshire

A complete catalogue is available from the publisher
at 3 Catherine Road, Newbury, Berkshire.

PUB WALKS
IN
County Durham

Charlie Emett

COUNTRYSIDE BOOKS
NEWBURY, BERKSHIRE

First published 1996
© Charlie Emett 1996

All rights reserved. No reproduction
permitted without the prior permission
of the publisher:

COUNTRYSIDE BOOKS
3 Catherine Road
Newbury, Berkshire

ISBN 1 85306 428 9

Designed by Mon Mohan
Cover illustration by Colin Doggett
Photographs by the author
Maps by Trevor Yorke

Produced through MRM Associates Ltd., Reading
Typeset by The Midlands Book Typesetting Company, Loughborough
Printed by J. W. Arrowsmith Ltd., Bristol

For my dear friends
Bill, Ron and Ellen
We walked the fields together

Contents

Key to Maps

Roads   Church

Tracks   Pub, Inn or Hotel

Railways   Bridge

Rivers   Tree

Buildings   Castle

Publisher's Note

We hope that you obtain considerable enjoyment from this book; great care has been taken in its preparation. However, changes of landlord and actual closures are sadly not uncommon. Likewise, although at the time of publication all routes followed public rights of way or permitted paths, diversion orders can be made and permissions withdrawn.

We cannot of course be held responsible for such diversion orders and any inaccuracies in the text which result from these or any other changes to the routes nor any damage which might result from walkers trespassing on private property. However, we are anxious that all details covering the walks and the pubs are kept up to date and would therefore welcome information from readers which would be relevant to future editions.

Area map showing locations of the walks.

Introduction

County Durham lies between the populated areas of Tyneside to the north and Teeside to the south. From the North Sea coast it unfolds westward into the Pennines, a rare blend of history, heritage and countryside. Whether your taste is for medieval, more recent social, or natural history, the area offers much to ponder over in its castles, its mining and farming communities. Covering 1,000 square miles, it is mainly rural, with sharp contrasts in the character of the countryside. It ascends from the low, wooded valleys along the coast, through rolling farmland, to the upper moors of the Pennines with all their wild beauty.

Three lovely rivers and their tributaries rise among the western heights. To the north, the Derwent flows through upland woodland, eventually to join the Tyne. The Wear, in the centre, curls round Durham Cathedral in a deep gorge; and, to the south, the Tees thunders over the impressive falls of Cauldron Snout and High Force before leaving the county downstream of Darlington.

The Durham dales, delightful Teesdale with its whitewashed farms, lovely Weardale and the environs of the Derwent, where its secrets are hidden in wooded hollows, belong to an Area of Outstanding Natural Beauty. High in these valleys, reservoirs lie like sapphires, the surrounding pastures edged with dry-stone walls. A delight at any time of the year, they are particularly beautiful when the surrounding trees wear their glorious autumn colours before stripping for their winter sleep.

Eastwards, the dales give way to lower hills and valleys. To the south the Tees flows across a wide plain, passing a proliferation of farms and villages. In this plain, castles and country houses, fields and parkland display the pageant of the county's history, set against a green background of neat fields and woodland.

Centuries of coal mining, which devastated much of the original beauty of the county, strongly influenced its character. Durham gained the reputation of being a wasteland of pit heaps and desolation. But today, thanks to the skill and care of the local authorities, much of the countryside's original beauty has been regained. Landscaping has healed scars and green, open spaces have replaced pit heaps. Resourcefulness and good husbandry have transformed the legacies of the Industrial Revolution into fascinating places that now harmonise with the environment.

There are twelve main towns in the county and only Darlington and Durham City contain more than 30,000 people. One of Durham's greatest assets is its inhabitants; and prominent in the local economy are the craft and cottage industries so often associated with farms and smallholdings in the dales.

To wander through the Durham countryside is a fine way of stimulating both your mind and body, and to this end these 20 short pub walks have been collated. Together they contain everything for the country lover – a landscape comprising some of the most impressive views in England, all manner of wildlife and stirring snippets of folklore and history. Moreover, the natives are friendly, and the publicans well versed in the art of satisfying the inner man.

All the walks have been chosen with the family in mind. None is too strenuous for anyone of moderate fitness, and the routes are unambiguous and easy to follow. The average length of 3 miles should not place a great burden on even the inexperienced walker – and so pleasing, diverse and interest filled are they that, often, the participant finds that the walk ends all too soon. Here the pub from which the circuit begins now comes into its own as disappointment is assuaged by the tempting fare on offer inside.

Not all pubs take advantage of the extended licensing hours. A rule-of-thumb guide is that opening hours are from 11 am until 3 pm and from 6 pm to 11 pm on Monday to Friday, from 11 am to 11 pm on Saturday, and from 12 noon to 3 pm then 7 pm to 10.30 pm on Sunday. Pubs with longer opening hours usually have a large banner to that effect prominently displayed.

The maps I have recommended are the ones I used because they were the ones I had. OS Landranger maps have a scale of $1\frac{1}{4}''$ to 1 mile and are adequate for all these walks. OS Pathfinder and Outdoor Leisure maps have a larger scale, $2\frac{1}{2}''$ to 1 mile, and give more detail. It is always advisable to supplement the sketch map with the relevant OS map.

This book's raison d'être is safely to guide adventurous, country loving enthusiasts through that part of England's green and pleasant land that is the 'Land of the Prince Bishops'. In the relaxed atmosphere of the 20 friendly inns featured here, walkers can savour the nectar and ambrosia on offer – though why anyone would choose creamed rice when sliced breast of duck in a blueberry and port dressing is on the menu beats me.

Slainte dhuitse (health to you) and good walking.

Charlie Emett
Spring 1996

Middleton-One-Row
The Devonport Hotel

1

Middleton-One-Row is magnificently sited, high on an embankment where the Tees, in its middle reaches, performs one of its magnificent bends. Hereabouts, the river is the county boundary and Middleton-One-Row, on the elevated Durham bank, enjoys a sweeping view across to a low-lying part of rural Yorkshire.

The Devonport Hotel stands in the heart of the village, overlooking picturesque countryside that extends to the Cleveland Hills. Formerly a row of cottages, the hotel dates back 300 years. This is a beautiful country inn and it has great charm. There are two restaurants as well as a lounge bar and a 'locals'' bar, all full of character. Outside seating is also available. Sixteen attractive en-suite bedrooms are on offer for a longer stay.

The Oyster Brasserie menu includes a good selection of high quality fish cuisine, such as fillets of Dover sole wrapped in smoked salmon with lobster sauce, swordfish steak with a sweet chilli sauce, grilled rainbow trout with anchovies and capers and fresh oysters served with lemon. Traditional pub grub is as diverse and exciting as Desperate Dan's real ale pie and oxtails in red wine and onions. More than a dozen oriental dishes are available – Malaysian prawn satay, Indonesian chicken nasi

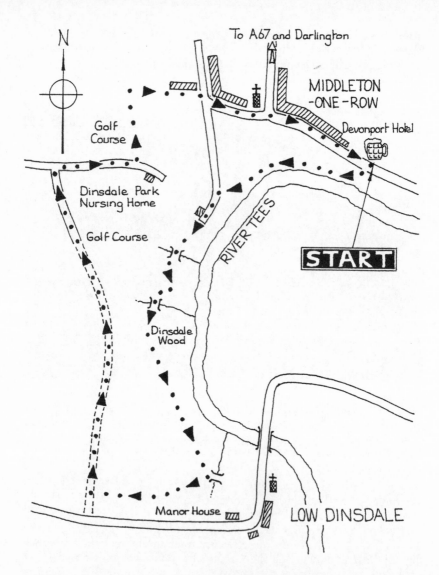

garen and a traditional Chinese lemon chicken stir fry, among them. All the bar meals, different pizzas and fresh sandwiches, using breads as varied as Greek datchula, bagels, brown, white and granary baguettes and available with fillings to suit all tastes, are also take-aways. Food is served between 12 noon and 2.30 pm and, in the evening, between 6.30 pm and 9.30 pm. To complement your meal there is a selection of over 80 wines

from around the world. In the bars the beers and ales are supplied by Newcastle Breweries, with real ales from Theakston and Marston's, and regular guests. The Devonport welcomes children and dogs.
Telephone: 01325 332255.

How to get there: Middleton-One-Row lies some 3 miles south-east of Darlington. Take the A67 eastwards from Darlington to Middleton-St-George, turn right at a junction in the village and follow an unclassified road southwards for 2/3 mile, where it turns sharp left into Middleton-One-Row. The Devonport Hotel is midway along the village street, on the left.

Parking: You can park on the hotel forecourt.

Length of the walk: 4 miles. OS map: Pathfinder 600 (inn GR 353123).

A panoramic view across the Tees to the purple hills of distant Cleveland adds an excitement to this walk which is maintained throughout its length. For the first 1 1/2 miles the route threads a thickly-wooded scarp in which, every spring, an explosion of wild flowers, primroses, violets, celandines, wood anemones and wild garlic, colours the undergrowth. The walk continues across lush fields and a golf course, mostly along paths and field tracks, always on clearly-defined rights of way.

The Walk

From the Devonport Hotel go diagonally right across the road to join the Teesdale Way at a footpath sign. Descend a bank on a path, stepped at the bottom, to the riverside. Turn right along another path, cross a waymarked stile and continue upstream into Dinsdale Wood. The path edges the river most pleasantly and reaches a surfaced road. Turn left along it, through a gateway, directed by a Teesdale Way sign, and continue, parallel to the Tees, soon to front a large house, where the road ends. Cross a facing stile and continue through woodland along a contouring path. Soon a feeder is crossed on a footbridge and, a little beyond it, the path climbs quite steeply, then levels for a short distance before descending, curving right, then left, to bridge another feeder.

As the path meanders pleasantly through the greenery, the Tees is glimpsed below, on the left, and fishing herons are often present.

Leave the wood over a facing step stile into a field. Cross this on a faint green path which passes to the right of a telegraph pole, beyond which bear left to reach a small concrete bridge over a ditch.

From here Low Dinsdale, a working village with lots of character, spreads itself between protective trees. Prominent is its pink sandstone church, surrounded by copper beeches. The oldest building, Dinsdale Manor House, dates mainly from the Tudor period but contains some 13th-century masonry.

Do not cross the concrete bridge. Instead, turn right and aim for another telegraph pole, clearly seen ahead. On reaching it, cross a waymarked stile in the fence immediately behind it. Turn right and edge the field ahead on rising ground, close to a hedge on your right. Exit over a waymarked stile in the right-hand corner of a facing fence. Turn right, along a clear track, edging the field close to a hedge on your right.

The further you walk along the track the more substantial it becomes, as it goes first alongside Dinsdale Wood, on the right, then edges a golf course, also on the right, before going straight into it. Keep straight ahead, still on the broad track, ignoring an arrow pointing right along a narrow track. Exit the golf course onto a minor road and turn right along it, directed by a footpath sign.

The road, a very quiet one, reaches Dinsdale Park Nursing Home on the right. At this point, where the road curves right, turn left, over a waymarked stile, into another area of the golf course.

Cross it, diagonally right, directed by a yellow arrow, passing, on your left, a deep pond and a small copse of oak trees. A little further on there is a seat, should you fancy a sit down.

Leave the golf course through a gap stile in the left-hand corner of a facing fence. Immediately, turn right along a path, close to a fence on your right. Leave the field through a facing gap stile and keep straight ahead, directed by a yellow arrow, still keeping close to the fence on the right. As you follow the path a yellow arrow on a post confirms your route. Leave the field over a facing stile to the left of a gate.

Keep straight ahead, now along a roadside footpath between dwellings. Soon St Laurence's church is passed on the left, at the road end. Go straight ahead along the road you have just reached, into Middleton-One-Row, soon to reach the Devonport Hotel.

2 Neasham
The Fox and Hounds

Low-lying Neasham hides behind a pleasant, grassed over flood barrier, its gardens, in season, a blaze of colour. Like the New English Hymnal it is a happy blend of ancient and modern. At its western end Neasham Abbey, an early 19th-century villa, stands near the site of a Benedictine nunnery, founded *c* 1156 and dedicated to the Virgin Mary. The triangular shelter at the foot of Neasham Hill to the east of the village was originally a pumphouse built in 1879.

A headless apparition is said to haunt the road between Neasham and Hurworth, the next village upstream – but if it is spirits you seek, you would do better to look no further than the Fox and Hounds, smack in the middle of Neasham. As its name implies, this inn is very rustic. Oak beams, rural prints and shelves awash with pewter tankards and plates all contribute to the rich, country theme.

Steaks, of best British beef, are a speciality here and they are hung for a minimum of 14 days, with the surplus fat removed, ready to be grilled to your liking. Fish courses include large cod in crispy batter, haddock fillets and salmon steak. Main meals, be it steak and kidney pie, ham and mushroom tagliatelle or lasagne – and there are many more – are all served with a choice of salad, vegetable, boiled potatoes, chips or rice. There are vegetarian dishes, omelettes, fresh cut sandwiches and most attractive meals for children. Food is served every day at lunchtime between 12 noon and 2 pm. In the evening it is available from 6.30 pm (7 pm on Sunday) to 9.30 pm. Thirst quenchers include Wards and Vaux Samson real ale, Blackthorn sweet and dry cider, Labatt's, Heineken and Stella Artois lager, Guinness and assorted soft drinks. Dogs on a lead are welcome in the garden, but not in the pub itself.

Telephone: 01325 720350.

How to get there: Neasham lies 2 miles south of Darlington. From the A66 outer ring road, driving eastwards, turn right at the first roundabout after bridging the main railway line, along Neasham Road. At its end turn left into Neasham. The Fox and Hounds is soon reached on the right.

Parking: Ample parking is available on and near the pub forecourt.

Length of the walk: 3½ miles. OS map: Pathfinder 600 (inn GR 325101).

This is an easy stroll through a delightfully varied landscape. The balance of arable fields and woodland is good and the views are surprisingly expansive for so little effort. The climbs are gentle, the hedgerows awash with flowers for much of the year and fallow deer are frequently seen.

The Walk

From the pub go diagonally right across the road and bear left along metalled Newland Lane, as waymarked. On leaving Neasham, the lane becomes an unsurfaced track that cuts through a strawberry field, bridges a stream and continues to Neasham Springs Farm, on rising ground ahead.

The track is mostly unenclosed, with only the odd tree alongside it at irregular intervals. It is easy to follow.

On approaching Neasham Springs, the track climbs and turns left to front the farmhouse, then turns right, between the house and farm buildings. It goes straight ahead, edging a field close to a hedge on the left. Soon the hedge becomes a fence and the first post carries a waymarker. Simply follow the track, which soon continues along a waymarked lane.

As progress is made, Low Maidendale Farm is clearly seen ahead, slightly to the right. The lane curves right, towards the farm. Just short of it, where a farm road is met at a tangent on the left, turn right, over a stile in the fence on the right. Go diagonally left across a paddock,

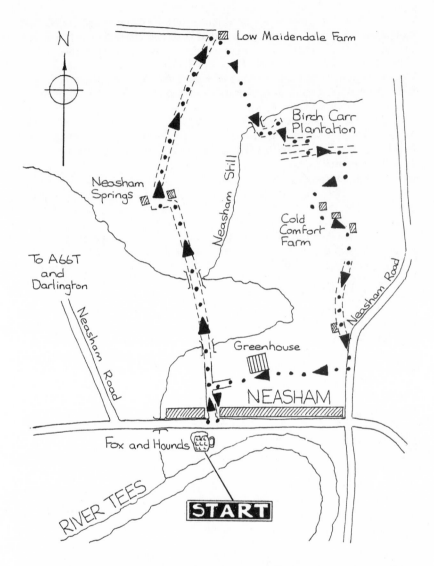

directed by a yellow arrow, and exit over a stile in a facing fence. Edge the field ahead, close to a hedge on the right, leaving over a footbridge that spans Neasham Stell at the right-hand corner of a facing fence.

Bear left, along a climbing path, through shrub, that turns sharp left and crosses a ditch, beyond which it turns right to the bank top. Here, turn left, edging the field, and descend to leave through a facing gate.

17

Immediately turn right, briefly edging a pasture, to cross a stile alongside a facing gate.

Follow a track along the bottom of a wooded slope on your left. It soon curves left through shallow Birch Carr Plantation, leaving over a stile to the left of a facing gate into a field. Continue, edging first a short fence, then a ditch containing some trees, on your right. Once past this ditch turn right and climb a slope, close to a fence on your right. On reaching a facing hedge, turn left, following a track until a gate in the hedge is reached. Turn right, through it, and edge the next field, close to a hedge on the left, with Cold Comfort Farm directly ahead.

Leave the field through a gate in the left-hand corner of a facing fence. Edge the next field, leaving through another facing left-hand corner gate. Now bear right to skirt the farm anti-clockwise, alongside a fence fronting a huge outbuilding. Stay with the fence until a facing waymarked stile is reached. Cross it, turn right and immediately cross another stile. Go forward, passing a house on the left, keeping straight ahead to descend a steep bank with a footpath sign at its foot.

Now bear left, briefly, to cross a stile into woodland. Continue diagonally right, directed by a yellow arrow, and bear right, following a clear path along the bottom of a wooded bank on your left. Soon a bungalow is passed on the right. Continue along its approach road to join Neasham Road at a tangent. Keep straight ahead, along a roadside footpath, for 100 yards, where you should turn right at a footpath sign, through a gap stile.

Edge the field ahead along an embankment capped with sandbags. Turn right at a facing fence, leaving the embankment, and bear left along a clear track, soon to pass greenhouses on the right. Go through a double gate and along a short tarmac road to a T-junction, where the lane used on the outward leg is regained. Turn left along it, briefly, retracing your steps to the Fox and Hounds.

Low Coniscliffe
The Baydale Beck Inn

3

Low Coniscliffe is a dormitory village, a neat rectangle of desirable residences set among low-lying fields with its back to the river Tees, hereabouts the haunt of fishermen. Exactly when the Baydale Beck Inn was built is not known but there has been something on the site for the past 400 years. In its early days the inn was famous for the gangs of thieves and rogues who frequented it, especially the cut-throat Cattons Gang. The robber Sir William Brown used it as his headquarters until he was tried and executed at Newcastle in 1743. It is thought that it is his ghost which still haunts the inn, although one Christopher Simpson was murdered there in 1624, so the ghost may be his. During the latter part of his career, Dick Turpin was supposed to have used the Baydale Beck, staying in a room with five doors for ease of escape. By 1824 the inn had become so notorious that the then landlord sold the property for 8 shillings.

Renowned as an ideal venue for families seeking good food and drink in a relaxed atmosphere, the inn, a Courage pub run by Wessex Taverns Ltd, has a family room, a beer garden and a play area for children. Well-behaved dogs are welcome in the beer garden, where water bowls are provided if requested, but not in the pub itself.

The most popular items on the menu are scampi, gammon, farmhouse grill, burgers, pies and salads. Cask conditioned ales include John Smith's Bitter and Magnet and Courage Directors. Scrumpy, Strongbow and Woodpecker cider are on draught. The inn is open from 11 am to 11 pm on Monday to Saturday, with the usual Sunday hours. Food is served between midday and 2 pm – the standard menu on Monday to Saturday and a special lunch on Sunday. Evening meals are available from 6.30 pm to 9 pm on Thursday and Friday only.

Telephone: 01325 469637.

How to get there: On leaving Darlington westwards, along the A67, within 300 yards of leaving the town the Baydale Beck Inn is reached on the right-hand side of the road. It stands alone, surrounded by fields, looking across the road towards the village of Low Coniscliffe.

Parking: There is a large car park to the rear of the inn.

Length of the walk: 3 miles. OS map: Pathfinder 600 (inn GR 254141).

Formations of pink-footed geese in noisy, gregarious flight can be seen during the winter months and green-headed male mallards and their dark brown mates, great crested grebes, whose feathers were once used to adorn ladies' hats, and tall, grey, sentinel herons, master fishers of infinite patience, bring thrilling spectacle to this gentle perambulation throughout the year. The outward leg is mostly along unsurfaced, riverside paths, much of the return being along a broad, clear track through fields. The scenery is a delight.

The Walk

At the walk's outset, before the A67 is crossed, a detour left of 300 yards will bring you to a most impressive undertaking, Northumberland Water's largest and latest water treatment plant. It cost £13 million and is open to the public from time to time.

From the pub cross the A67 and climb a facing stile into a field, directed by a footpath sign. Go diagonally right across the field, leaving through a facing stile at its right-hand corner. Edge the field ahead, close to a hedge on the right, leaving through a facing stile. Continue along a narrow lane, passing a dwelling on the left. At the lane end turn left, through Low Coniscliffe. In a short distance turn left, directed by a Teesdale Way signpost, and go between buildings towards the river. Turn right along a track that edges the river and at the end of it cross a facing step stile and continue straight ahead along an unclassified road. In a short distance the bridge carrying the A1(M), Darlington bypass, over the Tees is reached.

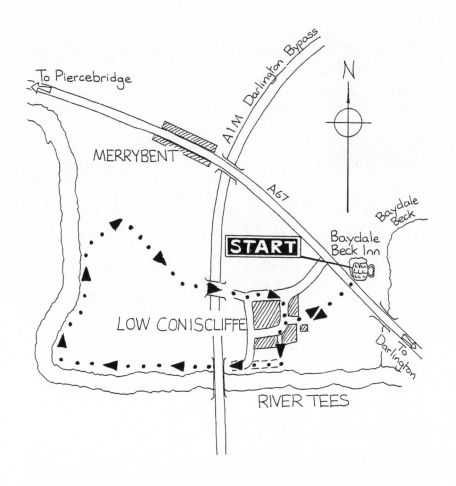

The ancient ford that crosses the river at this point links Low Coniscliffe on the north bank to another village, Cleasby.

Go under the bridge and follow a clear riverside path upstream. The Tees is ever close on your left and flat agricultural land is to your right. In about ¾ mile another clear path leaves the river at right angles – but do not take it. Instead, continue along the riverside path which soon curves sharp right with the river.

Cross a facing stile and continue upstream, edging the field ahead, only now with a flood barrier of earth between you and the river. At the end of the field cross a facing stile and continue, now on the flat top of the

21

By the river Tees at Whorlton.

barrier. The path slices through narrow woodland and goes through a gateway in a facing fence to continue alongside the river.

Where the path bifurcates take the right-hand one, up a bank, away from the river, to join, end on, a very clear field track. Follow this, leaving the river at right angles. It goes across a flat field, bending to the right in the middle of it, towards the motorway seen ahead.

Merrybent, another dormitory village, spreads along a ridge, over on the left; two rows of prosperous houses with the A67 between them. It is a pleasant spot but, like so many dormitory villages, has no focal point.

As you walk along the track, a public footpath sign on a post confirms your route. Follow the track, which reaches and crosses a bridge over the motorway, then descend to a large gate with a small one alongside it. Go through the small gate and immediately turn left along a tarmac road, edging Low Coniscliffe on the right. At the road end turn right, into the village, briefly. Where the road curves right, turn left at a footpath sign and retrace your steps to the Baydale Beck Inn.

4 Barnard Castle
The King's Head

Ancient Barnard Castle is a venerable town of great charm. It is set about its clifftop castle and two wide streets, Calgate and Market Street, lead from near the castle entrance at right angles to each other. Both are lined with 18th-century stone houses and an 18th-century market cross dominates the southern end of Market Place. Perhaps the most astonishing of all Barnard Castle's buildings is Bowes Museum, a magnificent 19th-century French château. Set in a 21 acre park, with gardens, tennis courts and a bowling green, it stares imperiously towards the moors of County Durham. A constant surprise, no matter how often you see it, the museum houses some 10,000 beautiful objets d'art in its 22 exhibition rooms, including paintings by El Greco, Goya, Boucher and Canaletto.

The original King's Head Inn was built in the mid-1680s, and in 1704 the Rose and Crown was sited next to it. In 1878 the Rose and Crown was demolished and rebuilt as part of today's fine, substantial King's Head. While Charles Dickens was researching *Nicholas Nickleby* he used the King's Head as his base, and this is celebrated in the many evocative sketches from his novels which grace the lounge walls. A plaque commemorating the author's visit, along with his illustrator,

23

Hablot K. Browne, in 1838, is also on view. Furthermore, the adjoining Charles Dickens Coffee Shop, which is open all day, shares the same owner.

The pub's reputation for the excellence of its food is as well established as is its Dickensian connection. The varied menu includes courses as varied and succulent as grilled rump steak and 'King's Head Special', a giant seven-inch Yorkshire pudding with fillings of roast beef, roast chicken, steak and Guinness and minced beef. There are senior citizens' and children's menus and a traditional Sunday lunch. Drinkers in this freehouse have a choice of Tetley Bitter, John Smith's Bitter, Burton Ale, Kilkenny Bitter and a guest ale. Castlemaine XXXX and Carlsberg Export lager, Guinness and Gaymer's Sweet and Addlestones Dry cider are also on draught. There is a garden area for children, a beer garden and a family room. Well-behaved dogs are welcome. Food is served on Monday to Friday from 11 am to 3 pm and 6 pm to 11 pm. On Saturday you can eat at any time between 11 am and 11 pm, and on Sunday from 12 noon to 3 pm and 7 pm to 10.30 pm.

Telephone: 01833 690333.

How to get there: Barnard Castle lies on the A67, some 15 miles west of Darlington. The King's Head is in the Market Place, on the right, close to the market cross.

Parking: Space on the site is limited, but there is a public parking area opposite the pub.

Length of the walk: 4¹/₂ miles. OS map: Outdoor Leisure 31 Teesdale (inn GR 048166).

This outstanding arboreal walk is a glorious blend of national and natural history. The town's castle, which has attracted writers and artists, including Scott, Turner and Cotman, dominates the skyline at the walk's start. One of the largest castles in the north, it enjoyed a chequered but largely peaceful existence. Guy de Baliol built it around 1100 and his nephew, Bernard, gave both the castle and the town his name. The Baliol family instituted the Oxford college.

The riverside path is pure delight, always close to the Tees, which flows, sometimes smoothly, sometimes in a turmoil of white spray, along a meandering course. The woodland is often alive with melodious bird song, flowers peep shyly from unexpected places in due season and there is a heady sense of freedom from mundanity.

The Walk

From the pub turn right along Market Place, passing the market cross on the left. As you go downhill a 16th-century house is passed on the left. Cromwell was entertained there in 1648 and, the accession of James II was celebrated by local magistrates. Turn right at a junction, along the A67, and where the road turns left over Barnard Castle Bridge continue straight ahead, along a climbing path.

The bridge dates from 1569 – the plaque says 1596 but this is incorrect – and until 1771 illicit weddings took place in the bridge's chapel.

Where the path bifurcates, go left, descending, then edging the river through woodland. Soon a pipe bridge is passed. Continue upstream on the clear path, curving right, briefly, then left, over a feeder, and returning to the river bank.

Slightly upstream of the feeder are six seats, favoured by ancients and young lovers alike.

The path rises, then contours, going between trees where, in springtime, primroses, anemones, bluebells and violets bloom. Where the path splits, go right, along the broader, ascending, one, with exposed roots and protruding stones making every step an adventure.

Having climbed some 300 ft above the Tees, the path fronts a stone buttress of a viaduct, now demolished, that once carried the railway line from Barnard Castle over Stainmore to Kirkby Stephen. It was one of the most scenic lines in the country. The views from here are magnificent and can be enjoyed from a well-sited seat. Because the land falls away steeply hereabouts and the drop is sheer in parts, people with children should keep them under strict control.

Once past the buttress, the path descends gently to river level and continues flatly through woodland. As progress is made, both the Tees and its edging path curve right. When the path forks, follow the left-hand, climbing, one, which soon descends along the foot of a cliff, back to river level. Here a flight of steps is met, which you go up. Continue along the path, edging an overhang. This is the stuff of adventure, like a scene from *Lord of the Rings*. Magical! Yet it is quite safe.

Soon the path widens, becoming a track, and here, where the river curves left and the vistas are superb, there is another seat.

Continue along the track and on reaching a junction follow the riverside option. Soon a yellow arrow on a fallen trunk confirms your route. Exit from the woodland through a facing, waymarked gate into a field. Edge the wall on your right until a small waymarked gate in it is reached. Go through it and climb the scarp on a stepped path, exiting through a waymarked gate into a field.

Immediately turn right, edging the field, close to a fence on the right. Exit through a facing, waymarked gate and edge the field ahead. Leave

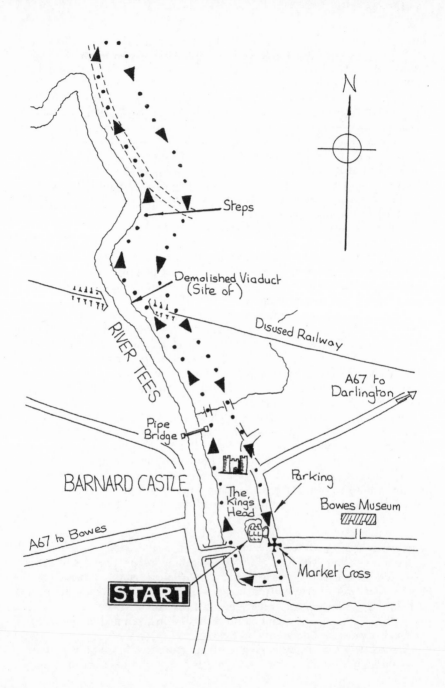

N

Steps

Demolished Viaduct
(Site of)

Disused Railway

RIVER TEES

A67 to
Darlington

Pipe
Bridge

BARNARD CASTLE

Parking

Bowes Museum

A67 to Bowes

The
Kings
Head

Market Cross

START

this one through another waymarked gate and cross the next field, still on the scarp's rim. On reaching a facing gate in a step in the wall on your right, go through it and follow a clear path, which offers stunning views.

Soon the path crosses the disused railway, close to the walled-up buttress on the right. Follow the higher of two paths, edging a fence on your left. Where it turns right, the path does likewise, descending and curving left, into a side valley. Turn left at a junction of paths, briefly, then right to bridge a feeder and climb a waymarked, stepped path.

On reaching a road, end on, go along it, using a footpath. Turn right at its other end, briefly, then left at a junction, going along a road which curves left short of the castle. At the road end, turn right, along Market Place, back to the King's Head.

5 Bowes
The Ancient Unicorn

Bowes is a quiet village on the eastern edge of expansive Bowes Moor. It stands where the Romans sited a fort, Lavatrae, to protect their route westwards, over wild Stainmore. The Normans built a castle there around 1175 to protect the English against invading Scots. Robert the Bruce destroyed it around 1322. Today only the keep and a grassy moat remain. Charles Dickens used one of the village's buildings as the model for the notorious Dotheboys Hall academy. It really was a school, whose head was William Shaw – he became Wackford Squeers in *Nicholas Nickleby*. In that famous novel, published in 1838, Dickens described the Ancient Unicorn as the place where the coach carrying the schoolboys stopped. He stayed there while he was researching the book.

Built in the 16th century, this substantial pub, on the western side of a cobbled square, has always been a coaching inn. One owner had a daughter, Emma, who was in love with a local boy, Edwin. Her parents disapproved, so they met secretly on Bowes Moor. Edwin caught pneumonia and died, and broken-hearted Emma lost the will to live. They were buried together in Bowes cemetery and Emma's spirit haunts the pub. Today it is enlightened visitors and locals who do most of the haunting, attracted by the relaxed atmosphere and the salubrious fare. Inside, a long, friendly-looking bar faces a large room, part of which is the dining area, the rest having tables for drinkers. Local farmers make frequent use of this homely hostelry, so the air is often thick with talk of farming matters and general chit-chat.

Scampi, pork or lamb chops and chilli con carne, all served with salad and chips, are examples of the food on offer. Younger Best Scotch, McEwan's Export, Theakston Bitter and Strongbow cider are the drinks on tap, and there is a wine list. The pub is open from 12 noon to 2 pm (3 pm on Saturday) and 6 pm to 11 pm, with the usual Sunday hours. Food is available throughout lunchtime opening, and from 7 pm until closing time. The Ancient Unicorn is residential, and has a beer garden and a play area for children; but no dogs, please.

Telephone: 01833 628321.

How to get there: From Barnard Castle take the A67 westwards for 4½ miles to meet the A66 as it bypasses Bowes. Go under the bypass and turn left, briefly, to a crossroads, where you turn right. As you climb through the village, the Ancient Unicorn is on the right.

Parking: You can leave your car on the pub's square forecourt.

Length of the walk: 5 miles. OS map: Outdoor Leisure 30 Yorkshire Dales, Northern and Central areas (inn GR 996135).

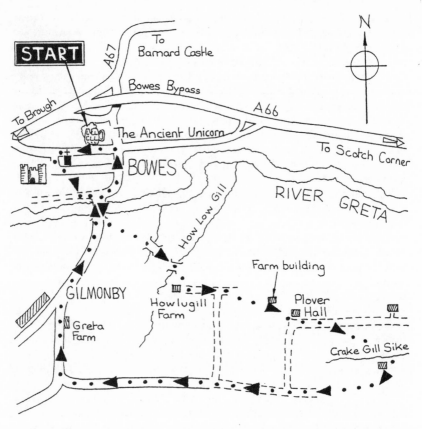

Plovers in erratic flight and the plaintive cries of gliding curlews can be as much a part of this easy but exciting walk as are the sheep and cattle in dry-stone-walled fields, the coarse grasses and heather of the open moorland and the sturdy hill farms that enhance its appeal.

The Walk

From the Ancient Unicorn turn right, through Bowes, passing St Giles church on the left. On reaching a 'Bowes Castle' sign, turn left, along a lane, passing the castle on the right. Soon the lane curves left, going between the churchyard and a cemetery. Just past the cemetery turn right, over a stile, directed by a footpath sign. Descend the field ahead diagonally left, exiting over a stile three-quarters of the way down the wall on the left. Continue diagonally right across the next field, exiting at a waymarked stile three-quarters of the way along a facing fence. Descend a bank on a narrow path, which curves left to join a track. Turn left along it, edging the river Greta, to an unclassified road. Turn right, bridge the Greta and in a short distance turn left, through a kissing-gate at a footpath sign.

Go straight ahead, crossing four fields, using clearly-seen stiles, the third one waymarked. Continue over a fifth field, at first close to a wall on the left, then bearing slightly right to cross a clearly-seen, waymarked stile in a facing fence.

Follow a clear path between trees, cross a ghyll on a footbridge, climb a bank and exit over a facing stile. Go diagonally right over the next field, leaving at the left-hand corner of a fence on your right. Immediately turn left, along a track, directed by a yellow arrow.

In a short distance the track crosses How Low Gill on an embankment over a culvert. Once over this feeder, turn right, directed by a yellow arrow, and go diagonally left up the field to the left-hand side of Howlugill Farm.

Turn left along a farm track, briefly. When the track turns right keep ahead, bearing right to leave the field through a facing stile. Cross the field ahead, exit over a facing stile and cross the next field parallel to a line

Bowes Village.

Old Mill waterfalls on the river Greta, below Bowes.

of trees on your right. Where the trees end, continue ahead, directed by a yellow arrow on a telegraph pole. Cross a narrow wood, go over a stile in a facing wall, beyond which there is an outbuilding. Go diagonally right to a tarmac farm road and turn left along it, passing Plover Hall Farm on the left.

Continue along this gated road and, short of White Close Hill Farm, seen ahead, go diagonally right, directed by a yellow arrow. Cross a rough pasture, aiming for a solitary tree, seen ahead to the left of a group of trees. On reaching this lonesome tree cross a stile in a facing wall, met at a tangent.

Go straight ahead, alongside a fence on your right, step over narrow Crake Gill Sike, climb a bank, pass to the left of West Ling Farm buildings and cross a stile in a facing wall onto moorland.

Go forward for a few yards and turn right along a green path, edging the moor. Keep left of a wood, then continue diagonally left, following the path along first a green sward between heather, then through the heather itself. There are some marshy bits here and there, which add to the fun and are easily circumnavigated if need be.

On reaching a waymarked gate in a facing wall go through it and continue along a broad green lane, which offers excellent views across the surrounding countryside. Where a fence crosses the green lane, go through a gateway in it. Continue along the lane, now following a tarmac farm road. When it curves right to join an unclassified road coming from the left, turn right along it.

Soon Greta Farm is passed on the right and some dwellings at Gilmonby on the left, just beyond which the signposted kissing-gate used on the outward leg is reached. Stay on the road, retracing your steps to the north side of the bridge over the Greta. Then continue to a crossroads, where you turn left into Bowes to find the Ancient Unicorn on the right.

6 Romaldkirk
The Rose and Crown

Throughout all England there are few villages prettier than Romaldkirk. Its lovely houses and quaint cottages are set about two well-kept greens, which still retain the stocks and a waterpump. The church of St Romald, 'the Cathedral of the Dale', has looked over it since Saxon days.

The Rose and Crown, which is still residential, was built in the days of coaches and four, in 1733, and its fabric remains much unchanged. The charms of the coaching days of old England endure in its panelled restaurant, crackling wintertime fire, in its copper and its brass.

A lunch at the bar might include smoked Loch Fyne salmon, followed by chicken livers, bacon and walnuts with salad and fresh pasta and, to round it off, a delicious home-made pudding. Perhaps you would prefer a chargrilled 8 oz sirloin steak with chipped potatoes and salad – there is plenty of choice. Food is available from midday to 1.30 pm and 6.30 pm to 9 pm throughout the week. A freehouse, the Rose and Crown has Theakston Bitter and Old Peculier on draught and the house wines include French red, French dry white and German hock. There are tables outside for alfresco drinkers, and, yes, children and well-behaved dogs are welcome.

Telephone: 01833 650213.

How to get there: Romaldkirk is 6 miles north-west of Barnard Castle on the B6277. Where the road edges the village, turn right, briefly, and the pub is on the left.

Parking: Adequate parking is available in the pub car park by the side of the building.

Length of the walk: 2½ miles. OS map: Outdoor Leisure 31 Teesdale (inn GR 995222).

The Tees enters one of its most attractive areas below Egglestone, near Romaldkirk. The walk edges the river at this spectacular part of its course, well away from any roads. So to see it, footwork is essential – and so very rewarding.

The Walk

From the Rose and Crown go diagonally left across first the road, then the village green, and turn left, along another tarmac road that fronts a row of cottages on the right. Soon the Kirk Inn is passed on the left. Just beyond it turn right, directed by a Teesdale Way sign, along a lane, between buildings.

The lane, pleasantly lined with tall trees, leads, straight and true, south-easterly. At the lane end go through the left-hand of two facing gates into a field with a small copse in that corner. Go through the copse and continue parallel to the wall on the right. Just clear of the copse a clear green path cuts across your line of walk. Turn left along it, soon to descend to a wicket in a facing hedge, which you go through. Continue diagonally left across the next field, still on a clear green path, to exit through a gap stile in a facing hedge. Descend a steep hill to join a track and go left, along it, as it curves right to pass in front of Low Garth on the left, beyond which you cross a facing step stile.

Immediately, turn left alongside the wall on your left and continue past it, bearing slightly right along a clear path towards the Tees. On approaching the wooded riverside, the path swings right and leads to a facing stile to the right of a gate, which you cross, into woodland. Continue, bearing right, along a clearly-defined arboreal path, parallel to, but at first out of sight of, the river, then edging alongside it.

Rushing along its rocky bed, a turmoil of white spray, then gliding smoothly across a dark dub, flecked with froth, to break into more rough water as it makes a spectacular change of course, the Tees rivals summertime campions and forget-me-nots, fungi and the silvan banks themselves. Together, these and other equally attractive components make a glorious whole.

The path rounds the bend of the river, descends to cross rocks and

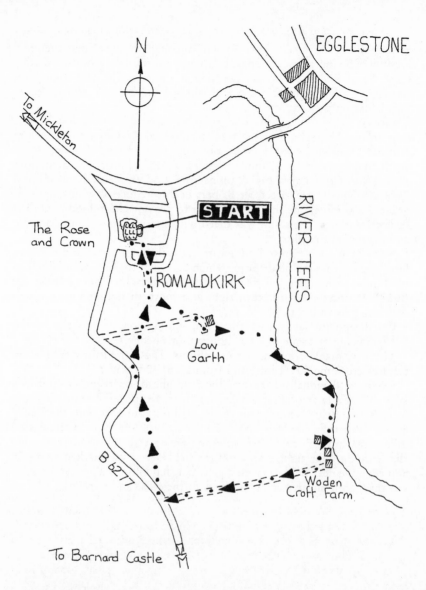

continues edging the river, a delight to walk and easy to follow. In a short distance it widens slightly and cuts a swath between lovely young trees to the foot of a bank.

From here, now gravelled and twice its original width, it goes up the bank, passing a Teesdale Way symbol on a post, which confirms your route. Near the bank's top, cross a stile and continue along the path for a few yards, where you go left, through a gate. Edge the field ahead, following a track alongside a fence on the left, towards Woden Croft Farm seen ahead. Leave the field at a facing stile, pass some farm buildings on the right and continue along a gravel track alongside the farmhouse on the left.

Woden Croft Lodge, the last building beyond the farmhouse, was once a boarding school of the type highlighted by Charles Dickens in *Nicholas Nickleby*. One famous old boy was Richard Cobden, who spent five years of his school life there. In 1839 he became a founder of the Anti-Corn Law League, pioneering modern methods of political agitation. The league forced Sir Robert Peel to reduce duty on imported grain to a nominal one shilling a quarter to provide cheap food for urban factory workers. The result was that English farmers could not compete and many had to sell up.

Short of Woden House Lodge turn right through a gate and follow a farm track across the field ahead, which bears left to edge woodland. On reaching a facing gate, go through it and turn right, briefly, along the B6277. In about 20 yards turn right at a footpath sign and go through a kissing-gate into a field.

Go diagonally left across the field, aiming for a step stile to the left-hand side of a gate in a facing hawthorn hedge.

There are many strip lynchets hereabouts. These prehistoric cultivation terraces are some 800 ft long and from 15 to 40 ft wide.

Continue diagonally left, over the field ahead, on rising ground to a step stile in a facing fence, which you cross. Keep in the same direction to cross a clearly-seen gap stile in the wall on your left, onto the B6277 again. Turn right along it and, where it curves left, cross a triangular, green area and go over a step stile in a facing wall. Continue alongside the fence on your right. Exit from the field over a waymarked step stile and edge the next field to reach a gate in a step in the wall on your right. Go through it and retrace your steps to the Rose and Crown.

7 Middleton-in-Teesdale
The Teesdale Hotel

Middleton-in-Teesdale developed as an agricultural settlement, became a market town and prospered as a lead mining centre when the London Lead Company, also known as the Quaker Company, became established there in 1815. With the decline of this industry, Middleton returned to agriculture and embraced tourism. Built in terraces and with two wide streets forming the letter L, it is a most attractive place, its snug stone cottages and large 19th-century houses blending well with the landscape. Middleton is ideally suited as a base from which to explore the myriad charms of Upper Teesdale. Exciting paths radiate from it in all directions – beside the Tees, uphill and down dale, through woodland, across fields and onto the rolling moorland along the valley's rim. The surrounding countryside, where sheep graze in high pastures, is renowned as a botanist's paradise.

The Teesdale Hotel is a 17th-century coaching inn located near the centre of this delightful little town, its fine, stone-built exterior exuding much olde worlde charm. But the pub has moved with the times. A stone archway through which horse-drawn coaches used to pass now leads onto a courtyard designed as a Spanish cantina. This more than compensates for the lack of a garden. All the bar meals are

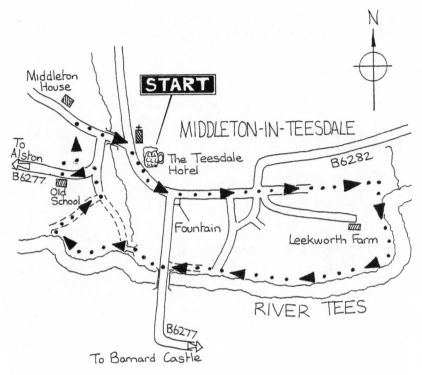

home-made and the menu includes exceedingly good steak and kidney pie. Another favourite is poached smoked haddock with egg and cheese sauce. Vegetarian meals unsurpassed throughout Teesdale are among the excellent food offered in the Coach House Restaurant. Lunch is served from 12 noon to 2 pm in both the restaurant and the bar and restaurant evening meals are from 7.30 pm to 8.30 pm, with bar meals from 7 pm to 9 pm, every day of the week. As for drinks, Burton and Tetley real ales, Old English cider and Carlsberg lager and Guinness are all on draught.

The atmosphere here is warm and friendly. Children are quickly set at their ease, and dogs are welcomed. Should the combined effect of the pleasant surroundings, the wintertime log fires, the superb food and the good ale prove soporific, well-furnished bedrooms with private bath are available.

Telephone: 01833 640264.

How to get there: Middleton-in-Teesdale lies some 9 miles north-west of Barnard Castle and 21 miles south-east of Alston, on the B6277. The Teesdale Hotel is on the right-hand side of Market Place when approached from the Barnard Castle direction.

39

Parking: You can leave your car at the rear of the pub, across the road from it, or in the car park to the east of Market Place.

Length of the walk: 3½ miles. OS map: Outdoor Leisure 31 Teesdale (inn GR 947255).

The history of lead mining and great natural beauty go hand in hand along this delectable walk. It is a short journey into Middleton's past, the going is easy and the way straightforward, mostly across fields and alongside the river Tees.

The Walk

From the Teesdale Hotel turn left, down Market Place. Ignore the junction on the right, at its end.

The handsome cast-iron fountain at this junction is a memorial to the London Lead Company and the benefits it brought. In 1877 employees subscribed to a retirement collection for Robert Bainbridge, the Company's Superintendent. Sufficient cash remained after buying him numerous presents to pay for this fountain and another at Nenthead.

Continue along Cattle Market to its eastern end.

Many houses in Middleton were individually built. The Company houses had hipped gable ends which gave the buildings eaves on four sides. Only the most deserving employees were housed in them. Just beyond the eastern end of Cattle Market, on the right, an ornamental arch, once filled with iron gates, marks the entrance to New Town, a Company development in which the larger houses with stables housed under-managers, surveyors and the doctor. The terraces, downhill, housed the more lowly, who had to be hard workers and sober.

Where the road curves left, keep straight ahead along Leekworth Gardens, between dwellings. Continue along a clear path across fields from where the retrospective view of Middleton is good. After ¾ mile, on approaching a little wooded ghyll, turn right, through a stile in a wall, and descend a meadow, exiting over a facing wall stile, directed by a Teesdale Way sign. Continue along a riverside path, soon to cross another facing, waymarked stile into a caravan site. Edge it, alongside the Tees on the left, and leave over a facing stile in the field's left-hand corner.

This section of the river is used for slalom canoe racing. The dipper which, because it has a white breast, is also called Betty White Breast is attracted to fast-flowing waters and frequently makes its home hereabouts. During the summer months sandpipers are ever present along this stretch of the Tees.

Continue upstream along the river bank, soon to join a partly cobbled path once used by miners walking to and from their places of work. Soon

County Bridge is reached but not crossed.

Built in 1853 by public subscription, this bridge replaced an earlier one dating from 1811, which collapsed before being completed. It was so called because until 1974 the river Tees was the boundary between Durham and Yorkshire. A local butcher, Richard Attee, regularly predicted the collapse of the earlier structure and eventually was proved right. While he was pointing out its defects to his wife, the partly completed bridge fell, killing them both.

Cross the road and follow a waymarked path upstream, soon to cross Hudeshope Beck on a footbridge. Immediately turn left, cross a stile and take the pleasant riverside path upstream. In a short distance, on the far bank, a feeder joins the Tees over a waterfall. The river makes a gentle curve right, then a more pronounced one left. At this point go through a facing stile and immediately turn right, briefly, to join the track. Turn left, along it, edging a wall on the right. Continue along a lane and at its end turn left along a broader one, briefly, to join the B6277. Turn left for a short distance and on approaching an old school turn right, across the road, and enter a waymarked lane.

The school, a Company school, was built in 1861 to replace a smaller one. Workers' children were taught there at a fee of one shilling per quarter. Many of the Company's managers, engineers and surveyors began their education there.

Turn right, along the lane, which soon turns left, edging parkland, and climbs to go between houses onto a minor road.

The prominent building on the far side of the road, diagonally left, is Middleton House, headquarters of the London Lead Company, which had such an influence on the town. By 1857 nine out of ten people in the area were connected with the lead mining industry.

Turn right, downhill, to rejoin the B6277, cross the bridge over Hudeshope Beck and continue along the road, soon to reach, on the left, the Teesdale Hotel.

Forest-in-Teesdale
The High Force Hotel

The impressive, stone-built High Force Hotel is situated in the unspoilt valley of Upper Teesdale, directly opposite an easily negotiated path to High Force, the country's highest waterfall. Constructed in the early 19th century by the Dukes of Cleveland as a shooting lodge, and looking for all the world like two buildings with identical gable ends facing the road, joined by a long central section, it would not be at all out of place on the Scottish Borders. It is now a family run hotel, with friendly bars, which are warmed by blazing fires in the winter months.

Among the main course dishes on both lunchtime and evening menus are griddled sirloin and gammon steaks, and baked rainbow trout and almonds, with accompanying vegetables and potatoes. Both menus tickle the tastebuds and there is much from which to choose – Yorkshire pudding filled with Teesdale sausages and gravy, perhaps, or a vegetarian meal such as a delicious mushroom and fettuccine hotpot. There is also a 'specials' board. Toasties, sandwiches and jacket potatoes are available as snacks, and children have their own menu. Lunchtime all week is from noon to 2.30 pm, while evening meals are served between 7 pm and 9.30 pm on weekdays and until 9 pm on Sunday. Drinks are served from 11 am to 4 pm and from 7 pm to 11 pm on Monday to Saturday,

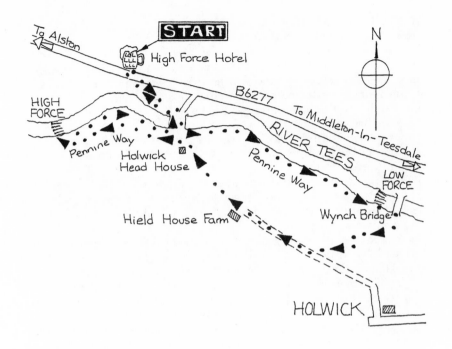

with the usual Sunday hours. This is a freehouse and the real ales include Theakston's full range and guest beers. Draught cider and wines are also available. The pub has a children's certificate for the whole of the premises, and there are picnic tables outside – and an ice cream kiosk. Dogs, however, are not allowed, not even well-behaved ones. Sorry!

Telephone: 01833 622222.

How to get there: The High Force Hotel stands in solitary splendour beside the B6277, 5 miles north-west of Middleton-in-Teesdale.

Parking: In front of the pub or in an adjoining public car park.

Length of the walk: 3½ miles, including a detour to High Force. OS map: Outdoor Leisure 31 Teesdale (inn GR 885286).

The whole of this area is a mecca for walkers, whether they are in search of a quiet ramble along the Tees or a more demanding trek. The riverside section of this route, which includes the falls at both High Force and Low Force, coincides with the Pennine Way, but all of it is easily walked.

The Walk

From the High Force Hotel go diagonally left across the B6277 and bear left along the roadside footpath, briefly, to a footpath sign, where you turn right along a stepped path, descending a wooded bank that edges the Tees. The steps have metal bannisters to ease progress. Exit the wood through a gate and continue downstream, edging a field along a green path. Go through a kissing-gate, turn right and cross the river on Holwick Bridge.

Immediately turn left for a few yards, go over a facing stile and continue downstream, crossing facing stiles until Low Force is passed and, just below it, the Wynch Bridge is reached.

Botanists drool over this part of the river, where grow the delicate pink bird's eye primrose, bog sandwort, yellow globe flower, rockrose, deep blue spring gentian and shrubby cinquefoil. At least 150 species of rare plants bloom hereabouts.

Low Force, also known as Little Force or Salmon Leap, is much favoured by visitors. Below this series of low falls the river surges through a narrow gorge and the current is dangerous.

The Wynch Bridge spans the gorge. Opened in 1830, it replaces an older one dated 1704 which was used by miners. Thought to be the first suspension bridge in Europe, it had a handrail on one side only and 'few strangers dare trust themselves' to cross it. In 1803 the main chain broke while some miners were crossing and one man was drowned.

From the Wynch Bridge take a path downstream, briefly, to a kissing-gate and continue along a clear path that curves right, away from the river. At the far end of a wooded bank on your right turn right, directed by a yellow arrow. In a short distance cross a section of broken wall, continue over the next field, passing a waymarker on a post, and keep straight ahead to cross a step stile, also waymarked. Edge the field ahead close to a wall on the right. Just past where the stream on your left turns left, do likewise to cross a small concrete bridge.

A proliferation of golden marsh marigolds, or king cups, adorns this area from March to July.

Go forward to join a farm track, at first alongside a wall on the left, to a ruin, where the track curves right to leave the field through a facing gate. Continue along the track to meet a gated farm road at right angles. Turn right along it, passing to the right of Hield House Farm and going through a facing gate. Continue close to the wall on the right, go through a gate at the right-hand corner of a facing wall and cross the next field, still close to the wall. Leave through another facing gateway. Cross the next field on a farm track, towards Holwick Head House, seen ahead.

Here heartsease, blues, yellows and two tone, carpet the route, at their best during June and July.

Go through a facing gate and where the track splits at the farmhouse,

The High Force waterfall on the detour from Holwick Bridge.

go right, descending to Holwick Bridge. From here a detour left, up a stepped path, to see England's highest waterfall is a must. From the farm just passed, the path's left fork fronts it. But this is not a right of way, hence the walk down to the bridge and the climb back up the hillside.

Follow a well-maintained path between junipers, soon to edge the gorge into which the river plunges over High Force. Extreme caution is needed on this section.

Its roar is heard long before you see this spectacular phenomenon. The river crosses a thick layer of igneous dolerite rock, known locally as whinstone, and descends 80 ft into a pool at the head of a wooded gorge. It is one of the most dramatic drops in the country. Part of the Upper Teesdale National Nature Reserve, 150,000 people visit it annually. Folk don't fall over it often – only once!

Retrace your steps first to Holwick Bridge, which you recross, then back upstream to the High Force Hotel.

9 Langdon Beck
The Langdon Beck Hotel

There are few lonelier places in County Durham than Langdon Beck, from where the road across Langdon Fell to St John's Chapel, in Weardale, is, at 2,056 ft above sea level, the highest classified road in England. The hamlet, comprising some isolated farms and smallholdings, a small church, a school, a youth hostel and a pub, is loosely scattered around Langdon Common, one of the wildest places in the country.

Across the road from the Langdon Beck Hotel there is another building, which used to be a coaching house. In 1887, when the present pub was built, the coaching house licence was transferred to it. With Cross Fell, the highest point in the Pennines, only a few miles away, the inn needs to be up to withstanding the ravages of a long winter – and it is. Stone-built and strong enough to shake off the worst of storms, it has a bar that is small and snug and a real refuge. The dining room is a much larger place, well able to seat a bus load of people at a time. This is a freehouse which specialises in providing good, wholesome food for walkers at reasonable prices. Beef casserole and dumplings, chicken curry and rice, vegetable lasagne, scampi, sausage, eggs and pizza, all with chips, and various sandwiches are always on offer. Food is served from 11.30 am to 2.30 pm on Monday to Saturday, and 12 noon to 1.30 pm on Sunday. It is also available between 7 pm and 9 pm each evening. Opening hours at the bar are from 11 am to 3 pm and 7 pm to 11 pm on Monday to Saturday and from midday to 2 pm and 7 pm to 10.30 pm on Sunday, and you will find Newcastle Best Scotch and Exhibition and McEwan's lager on draught. The pub has a beer garden and a garden area for children. Dogs are welcome, except in the bar.

Telephone: 01833 622267.

How to get there: The Langdon Beck Hotel is sited on the left-hand side of the B6277, some 9 miles north-west of Middleton-in-Teesdale, where the road makes a sharp right turn followed by a left-hand one, having crossed the bridge over Langdon Beck.

Parking: You can park on the pub's forecourt.

Length of the walk: 3½ miles. OS map: Outdoor Leisure 31 Teesdale (inn GR 854313).

On this splendid airy circuit in Teesdale's lonely upper reaches you have for company the magnificent heights of Cronkley Scar and Widdybank Fell, with its abundance of birdlife. The landscape is wild and exhilarating, but this is an undemanding and easily-walked route.

The Walk
From the Langdon Beck Hotel turn right along a minor road which edges Langdon Beck and, on reaching a confluence with Harwood Beck, turns right, alongside the latter. In a short distance, immediately after the road bridges Harwood Beck, turn left along a riverside path, downstream to Intake Farm.

Many Upper Teesdale lead miners were allowed by the local land-owners to claim enclosures on the edge of moorland as smallholdings. There were lots of them and they became known as 'intakes'. Farms with that name are quite common.

A ford crosses Harwood Beck just upstream of its meeting with Langdon Beck. Should the water level be low enough, and it usually is, you can eliminate the road walking to the bridge described above simply by crossing the ford.

The path goes between the farm and the beck into a small paddock, then turns left, briefly, to cross a stile back to the beckside. Turn right, at first on low-lying ground, then, as a steep bank rises ahead, go diagonally left, up it. Continue downstream, at first high above it, then descend gradually and continue along the bank to Saur Hill Bridge, where the Pennine Way is joined.

The Pennine Way, at its roughest and toughest, follows an exhilarating

48

Cauldron Snout.

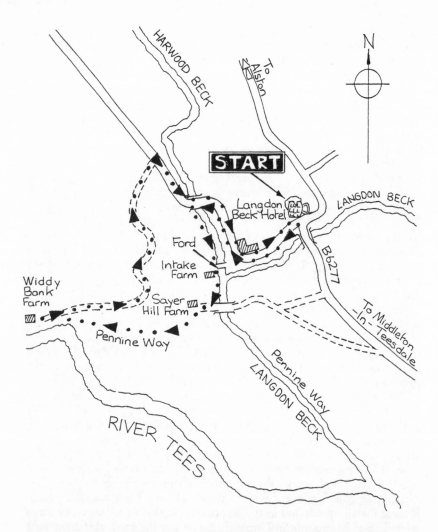

route through Upper Teesdale. The section this walk shares with it cuts through some real walking country between High Force and, upstream, Cauldron Snout. Heather-clad moorland, dominated by Cross Fell, is very close, to the west.

Turn right along the farm road to nearby Sayer Hill Farm and, on reaching it, bear left, as waymarked, on rising ground, which soon levels out, then descends slightly to a step stile in a facing wall to the right of a tree.

Go diagonally right across rough pasture, dropping at first, then climbing, to leave the field over a stile in a facing wall, close to a 'Nature Reserve' notice.

The bedrock over most of Widdybank Fell, prominent ahead, and Cronkley Fell, across the river, is either of the Lower Carboniferous Age, some limestone, some sandstone or shale, or is quartz-dolerite of the Great Whin Sill. As well as providing Upper Teesdale with superb scenery, the Great Whin Sill has formed the cliffs and rocky slopes, screes and riverside banks that are so important as habitats for many plant species which are unable to compete in closed vegetation.

Follow a green path, diagonally right, guided by marker posts, aiming for the as yet unseen Tees. On reaching the river bank, bear right to cross a stile in a facing wall and continue upstream to a second stile, beyond which go diagonally right to Widdy Bank Farm.

Here the Pennine Way is left to continue along perhaps its most exciting section, over the boulder strewn foot of Falcon Clints to Cauldron Snout two miles distant. This spectacular cataract falls in a series of eight steps. It is haunted, we are told, by the song of a local girl who, rejected by a lead miner who returned to his wife, threw herself into the foaming torrent. The sound is like that of a singing skylark.

The layout of Widdy Bank Farm is typical of many Upper Teesdale farmsteads. It is a Norse shippen with barn, byre and farmhouse all under one roof. Refreshments can be obtained here, but should they not be required, do not enter the farmyard. Instead, turn right, along the farm road, which skirts Widdybank Pasture, at first in a north-easterly direction, then taking a mean northerly route.

More than 83 species of birds have been recorded as nesting in and around the Upper Teesdale Nature Reserve of which Widdybank Fell is a large part. Perhaps the easiest to recognise is the red grouse, a game bird. Yet during the nesting season there is probably no area in Britain that harbours such a variety of waders as this wild and wonderful upland. The most common is the lapwing, but the curlew, with its liquid call, the drumming snipe, the common sandpiper, which has a trilling chatter, the golden plover, oyster catcher and redshank are all at home in these marshy fields and in the wet places on the higher fells. All three wagtails nest commonly in Upper Teesdale but the most abundant bird is the meadow pipit.

In just over a mile, at the farm road's end, turn right along a minor road, soon to edge Harwood Beck on the left, then cross it on the bridge used on the outward leg (if you didn't cross at the ford). From here retrace your steps to the Langdon Beck Hotel.

10 Hamsterley
The Cross Keys Inn

Of all the places in County Durham only majestic Durham Cathedral is a greater tourist attraction than Hamsterley Forest. Within its 6,000 square acres there are at least 60 species of tree, broadleaves and conifers. A few miles north-east of this magnificent mixed woodland, which is home to red squirrels, pipistrelles and all manner of wild creatures, is pleasant Hamsterley village. Surrounded by open country-side, its delightful dwellings form a long street set above a slanting village green.

The village pub, the Cross Keys Inn, is a snug haven where dominoes and darts can be enjoyed in a lounge graced with shining brasswork and polished woodwork. Bar meals are always available, and the 60 seater restaurant is very attractive. A comprehensive menu includes peppered sirloin, poultry dishes like 'South Sea Island Chicken', vegetable Provençale and fresh, crispy salads. Meals are served every lunchtime and evening, with special Sunday lunches. John Smith's and Stones Bitter, Beamish stout, Scrumpy Jack cider, dry German white and medium French red wines are all on draught. There is a beer garden, and swings and a slide are available for children. Dogs should remain outside.

Telephone: 01388 488457.

How to get there: Take the A68 northwards from West Auckland, turn left at High Etherley, still on the A68, and after 2½ miles, just short of bridging the river Wear, turn left, as signposted, to Hamsterley and within 2 miles there you are. The Cross Keys Inn is on the right, just beyond the village green.

Parking: There is a large car park behind the pub.

Length of the walk: 3½ miles. OS map: Pathfinder 580 (inn GR 117311).

With the great forest of Hamsterley stretching into the far distance to the south-west and elsewhere open countryside spread like a patchwork quilt, with nary a hint of the industry of Witton Park and Toft Hill only a few miles away, it is not surprising that this most pleasing of field and lane walks is so popular.

The Walk

From the Cross Keys turn left, briefly, then left again, between dwellings, directed by a footpath sign. In a few yards go over a stile to the left of a facing gate into a field, which you cross along a green path. Exit through a metal gate in a facing fence, go down the middle of a long, narrow field and continue along a broad, green lane. Exit through a facing, waymarked gap stile into a lane. Turn right along it and in a short distance go through a facing gate into Adder Wood and continue along the top of a wooded bank. Once there must have been adders here, but not any more – you are quite safe!

From this lane, to westwards, can be seen Bedburn, home to Dr David Bellamy, the famous naturalist.

Soon the track curves left and descends to the wood's edge. From here go diagonally right across the facing field towards a gate in the fence on the right. Do not go through it. Instead, turn left and descend the field, close to the fence on your right. On reaching the field's right-hand corner, go right, through a waymarked gate at the bottom end of the fence on your right. Edge the next field briefly to reach a tree which stands proud of the fence on your right, where you turn left, straight across the field, following the route of a culverted water course. The way is indistinct at first but becomes clearer as the field is crossed.

A line of trees edging Bedburn Beck spreads across your line of walk at the field's far side. Simply aim for that. Exit through a waymarked gap in a facing fence and turn right, along a woodland track, with Bedburn Beck on your left. Soon the track leaves the wood, continuing downstream, past a private bridge, where a clearer track is joined. Continue along it, go through a facing gate and turn left, directed by a blue arrow, along

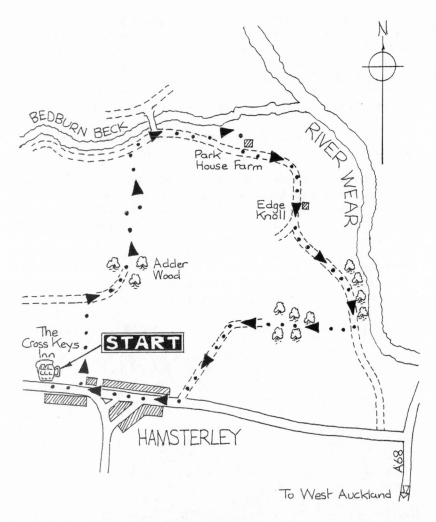

a clear path, at first alongside the beck, then curving right and climbing through woodland. Cross a lawn, a right of way, and go through a facing gate to reach Park House Farm.

Bear left, between dwellings, and continue along a farm road through some very scenic country, lush and green and well endowed with hedges and trees. The farm road curves left then sharp right, soon to nudge Edge Knoll farm on the left, where it curves right.

Watch out hereabouts for yellowhammers – they will warm your heart.

Where the farm road splits, take the left fork, which soon curves right, climbing alongside narrow woodland on the left, beyond which the river Wear flows. Just past some gorse bushes on the right, turn right, along an uphill path and go through a facing gate. Continue along a sunken lane, edged with hawthorns. At the lane end keep straight ahead, pass a solitary ash and follow the remains of a hedge, passing a second lone ash tree. Continue in the same direction to go through a facing gate into woodland.

From here the retrospective view is of a rural landscape untouched by any industry except agriculture.

Follow a climbing path through woodland which quickly thins and becomes heath. Soon the path enters a walled lane and begins to level out. The walls end and become a mix of hedge and fence.

As Hamsterley looms large ahead, the lane makes a beeline for it. At the lane end go through a facing gate and edge the field ahead close to a hedge on the left, which gently eases to the left. Now you have bungalows on your right. Leave the field through a facing gate and turn right, along the tarmac road, through the village and back to the Cross Keys.

11 Witton-le-Wear
The Victoria

Mellow Witton-le-Wear is sited halfway up a hillside, around which a railway curves. It contains many houses of character and its narrow, tree-studded green is squeezed between split-level streets. There is a pele house, Wilton Tower, at the west end of the village, clinging to the remains of a medieval manor house. The church of St Philip and St James rises above the higher street, the Victoria adorns the eastern extremity of the lower one.

There is something reassuring about this inn, a building of substance at the end of a row of stout, stone dwellings. Ivy climbing up the walls and large, inviting windows, behind which short, scalloped curtains allow peeps, tempt further investigation. Step inside with confidence to find friendly service, and a large choice of meals. Everything here is cooked to order. Should you desire battered mushrooms or wild boar pâté for starters, a T-bone steak weighing 16 oz uncooked and served with all the trimmings, half a roast duck or biryani, a slightly spiced Indian dish, all these and more are available. If you would prefer an open sandwich, a 'Hot Stottie', it is tasty and filling. Each day except Saturday, food is served from 12 noon until 3 pm. On Monday to Friday evenings, meals are from 6.30 pm until 11 pm, and on Sunday from 7 pm until 10.30 pm.

On Saturday food is on offer all day, from 11.30 am until 11 pm. For quenching a thirst there is a choice of 13 different draught ales available at the bar, Thorne Best Bitter, Vaux Bitter and Vaux's Waggle Dance among them. Scrumpy Jack and Woodpecker ciders are also on draught, and there is an assortment of wines. From the beer garden at the rear the land falls away to a shelf where there are children's swings. The land then falls away again. Dogs are welcome outside, but not in the pub itself.

Telephone: 01388 488501.

How to get there: Witton-le-Wear lies between Crook, to the north, and West Auckland. From the roundabout on the A689, 1½ miles west of Crook, take the A68 southwards for about 3 miles. Turn left, as signposted, into Witton-le-Wear and the Victoria is at the eastern edge of the green, on the right.

Parking: You can park at the rear of the Victoria.

Length of the walk: 3 miles. OS map: Pathfinder 580 (inn GR 148312).

The unrestrained power of water is terrifying. Banks are burst and top-soil is washed away when rivers in spate shake free from their confines. Man's efforts both to repair damage to the banks of the Wear, and to improve on the original, are clearly seen on this fine walk. Even without the flood prevention activity this circuit is a delight and full of merit, offering wide views of the surrounding area from the fields above the village.

The Walk

From the Victoria turn right along a roadside footpath. Just past the last house on the right, turn right along a concrete path, cross a facing stile and descend steps. Go over a railway line, diagonally left, exiting through a gap stile. Descend a bank on a clear path, cross the cricket field ahead, going behind the pavilion, and on reaching a fence turn right, alongside it, with the river Wear on your left. Leave the cricket field through a kissing-gate at the left-hand corner of a facing fence and continue along a riverside path.

Across the river, set back from it, is 14th-century Witton Castle, built by Sir Ralph Eure. Both the keep and the curtain wall are original. Much of the remainder is 19th-century, but in medieval style.

Soon a twin-arched old coaching bridge is reached. Cross the road alongside it, go through a waymarked gap stile and immediately turn right, along a path, towards a building, leaving the boulder-reinforced river bank. When the path ends, turn right, briefly, then left, going in front of a wooden building. Continue, bearing slightly right, past the

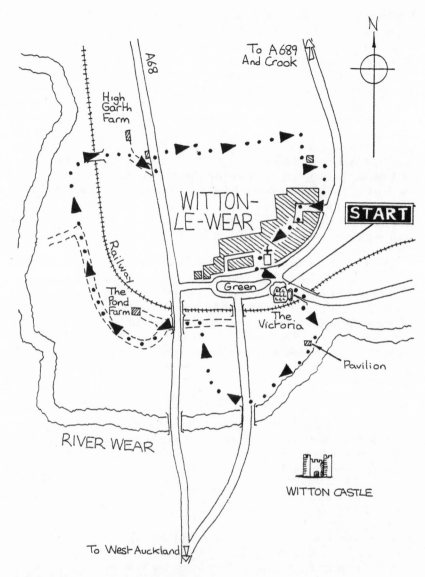

left-hand side of some trees, to cross a stile in a facing hedge. Go over the field ahead, bearing right, to cross a waymarked stile in a facing fence to the right of an ash tree. Go diagonally right across the next field, guided by a notice in the fence ahead, fronting a wooded bank. As you move towards the notice, a stile comes into view. Cross it, go over a boggy area on stepping stones and continue through a facing stile onto a farm road. Turn left, along it, going under the Witton-le-Wear bypass. Cowslips in profusion grow near this undercut in the spring.

Where the farm road splits, go left, through a gateway, curving right to edge a field. The track leaves the field at the right-hand corner of a facing fence and continues, edging the next field, passing The Pond Farm on the right.

Where the hillside on the right becomes wooded and the track turns left, continue along the foot of the hill. About 150 yards short of the end of the field, turn right along a path, going diagonally left, up the wooded bank. Exit over a step stile in a facing fence into a field, which you cross, bearing left. Leave it over a waymarked stile and continue over the railway bridge ahead. Immediately cross a step stile to the right of the right-hand one of two gates. Keep ahead, alongside the fence on the left, towards High Garth Farm. As you cross the field, bear right, to exit at a clearly-seen stile in a facing fence. Immediately turn right along the farm road.

On reaching the A68 turn left, briefly, and cross it, to go along a short access road to a field, which you enter to the right of a gate. Climb to a clearly-seen facing stile, which you cross. Edge the meadow ahead, close to a mix of hedge and fence on the right. Exit through a kissing-gate in the right-hand corner of a facing hedge. Go straight ahead, directed by a yellow arrow, turn right at the field corner and edge it, passing a farmhouse on the left. Leave through a gateway, turn left to the field corner, then right, down the field, alongside a wall on the left. Exit at a facing step stile.

Turn right, briefly, then left, along a raised footpath fronting houses. Descend steps, turn right along a quiet road, and take the first left down a cul-de-sac. Leave from its bottom right-hand corner, along a lane that leads through the churchyard, exiting at a right-hand corner stile. Turn left, along the front of the church, then turn right, across the road, and go diagonally left, back to the Victoria.

12 Escomb
The Saxon Inn

Escomb is renowned for its tiny Saxon church, which the *Collins Guide to English Parish Churches* calls 'after Durham Cathedral, the most impressive ecclesiastical building in the county'. It is an odd building, tall and narrow with irregular windows. Some of the stonework, taken from the Roman fort at Binchester, is encrusted with diamond broaching and other strange features.

Overlooking the church from across the road is an unpretentious pub, the Saxon Inn, once small, like the church, but now greatly, and sympathetically, extended to allow for tables at which bar meals can be eaten in comfort. All the food on offer is freshly prepared, with steak and kidney pie and lasagne regularly topping the popularity list. Meals are served from 11.30 am to 3.30 pm on Monday to Friday, 11.30 am to 4.30 pm on Saturday, and 11 am to 4.30 pm on Sunday, when lunch is a traditional roast, either pork or beef. The good choice of draught beers available includes Whitbread Best Scotch, Trophy Bitter, and Boddingtons. Lager lovers will find Heineken and Stella Artois. Children are allowed inside, and there is a play area for them outside. Dogs are welcome in the beer garden, if tied up, but not in the pub itself. Provided walkers purchase drinks, they may eat their own food – but it

is expedient to sample the pub fare because it is rather good.
Telephone: 01388 662256.

How to get there: Escomb has only one road leading into it. The most direct way there is from Bishop Auckland. Take the B6282 westwards from the town and on reaching a crossroads just clear of its outskirts turn right, northwards, for ³/₄ mile. As the road descends towards the church, the Saxon Inn is the last building on the left.

Parking: There is a car park at the rear of the pub.

Length of the walk: 2¹/₂ miles. OS map: Pathfinder 580 (inn GR 189301).

The riverside section of this interesting and informative walk abounds in birdlife and is along part of an old track from Escomb to Bishop Auckland once used by the prince bishops of Durham on their way to their Deer Park in Weardale from their palace in Bishop Auckland. The route then climbs up the valley side to gain a fine retrospective view of the Wear and a distant one-time railway viaduct. Back in Escomb, the marvellous little church is well worth a visit – for anyone wishing to absorb something of the piety of the age of Bede, this is the place to be.

The Walk

From the Saxon Inn turn left, briefly, to the road junction, where you turn right, passing the ancient church on the left. As the road curves left, do likewise, along it. Turn right at another road junction and go along a road which soon curves left. Just past some houses on the left, where the metalled surface ends, turn right, through a waymarked gate. Go along a field track which leads to a stile in the right-hand corner of a facing fence, which you cross. Keep straight ahead along a path which soon curves left to the river Wear, where you turn right, over a facing stile.

Continue along the river bank on a clear green path, crossing four fields, using stiles. Migrants like swallows, swifts and martins are a common sight here in summer. Mayflies, on which they feed, are the attraction – there are millions of them, in dancing clouds, overhanging the water. Other often seen birds are skylarks, sandpipers, magpies and goosanders.

Whenever the bishops of Durham, their guests and servants walked this 'Bishops' Path' alongside the Wear to holiday at Deer Park, some two miles distant, the inhabitants of Escomb had to become an advance party to build a palisade around the Hall and prepare the toilets.

Soon a feeder is crossed on a waymarked footbridge, beyond which you turn left, along a path, through scrub.

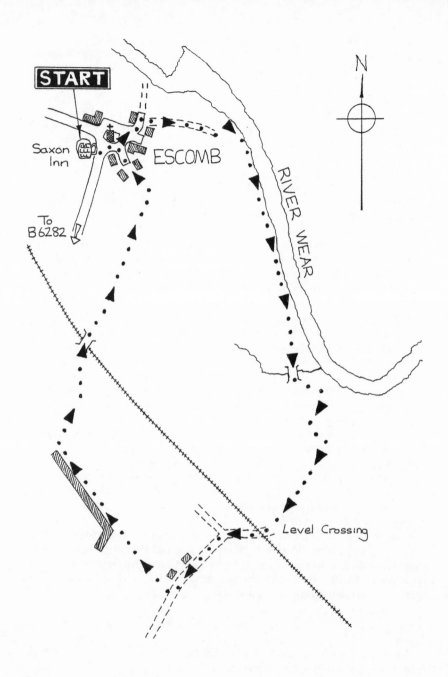

START

Saxon
Inn

To
B 6282

ESCOMB

RIVER WEAR

N

Level Crossing

The water below the bridge contains iron salts which change colour to bright orange when coming into contact with air. It is not poisonous. It is an outflow from a nearby drift mine at Pity Me. This gorse-covered hillside was once mined by digging into seams running into the sloping ground. The mounds are spoil heaps.

In a short distance the path curves right and climbs quite steeply, curving left and contouring to reach a stile in a facing fence. Cross it and immediately turn right, uphill, close to a fence on your right. The path, easy to follow, climbs above the scrub and offers excellent views up and down the river. The former railway viaduct in the distance was converted to carry a brand new road.

On reaching a stile in a facing fence, go through it, cross a railway line and follow a clear path, close to a fence on the left. The path curves right, then left, through a gateway into a lane. Go along the lane, passing a junction on the right and climbing steadily. At its summit, the track ends at a tarmac lane which passes three dwellings on the right. Go past them and continue beyond a lane end on the right, just after which, past another dwelling, you turn right, over a waymarked stile.

Keep straight ahead, crossing a field alongside a hedge on your right. Exit over a waymarked stile in the right-hand corner of a facing fence. Cross the next field close to a corrugated metal fence on the left. Go over a rough pasture, parallel to houses on the left, soon to join a path at a tangent and continue along it. The path goes along a lane with a high fence on the left and a hawthorn hedge on the right.

On reaching a crossing of paths turn right, briefly, along another path into a field, which you edge, still on the path. Leave through a gateway and continue down the next field. Leave this one over a waymarked stile in the left-hand corner of a facing fence. Cross the railway line on a bridge. 'Cement trains' from Eastgate, near Stanhope, used this line daily until recently.

Go forward, across a short field, leaving over a stile, left of a gate, and descend a large field on a clear green path. Leave the field through a stile in a facing fence and continue downhill, on the path, until a post carrying a bridleway sign is reached.

Turn left, for a short distance, then cross a facing, waymarked stile. Edge the field ahead close to a hedge on the right. Exit through a gap stile. Go along a footpath between dwellings and on reaching a road junction in front of the church turn left, briefly, and left again. The Saxon Inn is on the right.

13 Wolsingham
The Black Bull Inn

The little town of Wolsingham lies in a very pleasant setting at the eastern approach to Weardale. Its industrial side does not intrude and it has many attractive buildings. Whitfield House, for example, on the main street, is a fine, 18th-century, three-storey structure set back from the road, behind two ilex trees. Whitfield Place, next to it, is long and low, with mullioned windows, and is dated 1677.

The Black Bull Inn, built in 1720, was originally an excise office. Today its most popular custom is darts. It is residential and two of its guests are permanent – one is a benign ghost, the other his phantom hound. The ghost has a penchant for tapping shoulders and blowing into people's ears. Recently, the phantom hound dragged a guest from his bed so roughly that the man broke his arm. Who says all spirits are in bottles?

The pub, which faces the market place across the A689, is a whitewashed building, its windows having dark stone surrounds. In a welcoming, olde worlde atmosphere the inner man is cared for on Monday to Saturday from 11.30 am to 2.30 pm and 6.30 pm to 9.30 pm. Be it 'Roast of the Day' with Yorkshire pudding and seasonal vegetables, pork korma or a vegetarian dish like cheese and onion quiche, the food is delicious and the plate loaded, which does not mean that you have to be – the prices are most reasonable. There is a children's menu and assorted sandwiches are sold at the bar. On Sunday a traditional roast lunch is served between noon and 2 pm. The pub is a Vaux house and the most popular drink is hand-pulled Double Maxim. Vaux Samson, Lorimer's Best Scotch, Heineken lager, Scrumpy Jack and Woodpecker sweet cider are all on tap. Well-behaved dogs are welcome and on a fine day drinkers can watch the passing scene from the small beer garden that fronts the pub.

Telephone: 01388 527332.

How to get there: Wolsingham is on the A689 some 14 miles west of Durham City. The Black Bull Inn is on the left, facing the market place, as you go westwards up the dale.

Parking: You can park in the market place, directly across the road from the pub.

Length of the walk: 4 miles. OS map: Outdoor Leisure 31 Teesdale (inn GR 077371).

Elephants stamping along the valley's southern rim, trunk holding tail – that is what the famous elephant trees portray. They are seen to advantage from this exhilarating but easy walk through one of Weardale's most fertile parts. Nowhere in the dale is lusher than around Wolsingham, and it shows.

The Walk

From the pub turn left, along the road, crossing to its right side. Just past a road junction on the left, turn right along Church Lane. At the lane end continue through the churchyard, turning left at the church to a crossing of paths. Turn left, briefly, then right, through a gateway. Go along a lane edging the churchyard and continuing beyond it, past a junction on the right, to reach, but not to go through, a kissing-gate. Instead, turn left, still on the lane. At its end, go through a kissing-gate, then diagonally right, along a field path. Go through a kissing-gate, left of a gate in a step in the fence on the left. Continue along a lane beneath a copse of beech, chestnut and the odd Scots pine. Soon a minor road is crossed. Continue along the lane, signposted to Leazes Farm.

The elephant trees really do look like elephants from here.

The lane goes to the right of the farm and soon turns sharp left. Just before this happens, go right, through a waymarked kissing-gate, and immediately turn left. Continue along a bank above Ladley Burn on the right. Soon a faint path develops. It quickly curves right and descends,

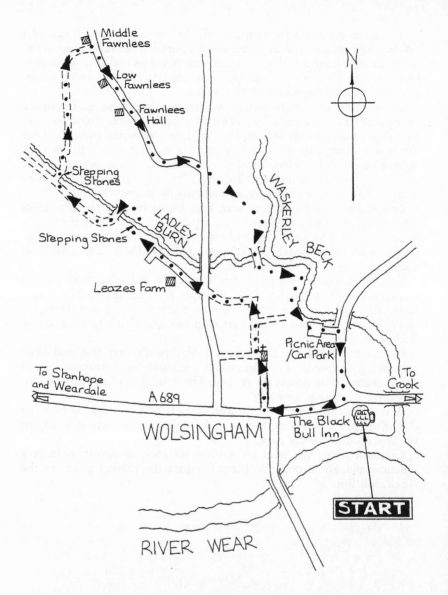

becoming broader. Cross a waymarked stile left of a facing gate and go over the stream on stepping stones. Immediately go left, upstream, along a green track, directed by an arrow. Climb a stile to the right of a facing gate into woodland. Recross the stream on a footbridge and follow a lane, which curves right, edging woodland on the right.

It is a lane to warm the heart, essentially rural. Come in spring and you will see, on one side, an infant stream, gurgling between dusky trees, bluebells an indigo coverlet, spangled with cowslips and pale primroses, on the other, fat cattle cud-chewing in green pastures and sheep gently nibbling, blissfully unaware of mint sauce.

On reaching a junction, turn right, down a short lane, go through a facing gate and again cross the stream on stepping stones. Go diagonally right, up a facing bank, and edge the field on a climbing track. Leave it through a facing gate and edge the next one, close to a wall on your right. Exit through a waymarked gate, pass Middle Fawnlees on the left and go through a gate into a walled lane. The long view down the valley is absolutely glorious, with greens and browns of every hue.

Turn right, along the lane, passing, first, Low Fawnlees, then Fawnlees Hall, soon to reach a minor road, which you cross. Go through a kissing-gate at a footpath sign and edge the field ahead close to a hedge on the right. Exit through a kissing-gate and edge the next two fields on a clear path to reach Waskerley Beck.

Turn right, along a beckside path, soon to cross Ladley Burn near its confluence with Waskerley Beck. Go over the field ahead. Exit over a facing stile and continue downstream on a green path. Leave through a facing kissing-gate into a long, narrow picnic area that edges Waskerley Beck.

Here, one spring, I came across a blackbird's nest that had been attacked, probably by a magpie, which are numerous hereabouts. Dead chicks were strewn across the ground. This is all part of nature and is to be expected on country walks.

Bear right, through the picnic area, to a car park, continuing between it and the beck, following a clear path, which soon meets at a tangent the approach to the car park.

Continue along the road for a short distance, then turn right at a junction and go through Wolsingham, past the market place, to the Black Bull Inn.

14 Stanhope
The Queen's Head

Remind the people of Stanhope that it is the 'capital of Weardale' and, with justifiable pride, they'll purr like kittens. For this beautiful town, which became wealthy on lead mining, is surrounded by lovely scenery, much of it woodland. Its parish church of St Thomas the Apostle, built around 1200, has a Roman altar in the vestry inscribed 'silvano invicto sacrum', sacred to the unconquered god, Silvanus. He was the god of the woods. Near the churchyard entrance is a fossilized tree stump which is 250 million years old.

The Queen's Head is not quite as ancient. It is a fine, stone-built town pub dating from the 1800s, with an underground arched cellar, just the place for keeping real ales. Window boxes, gay with colourful flowers during the summer months, adorn the first and second floor windows. This is a friendly, unpretentious hostelry, second home to many local people. All the food is fresh daily, and very tasty it is, too! Shortcrust steak and kidney pie, lasagne verdi and large Yorkshire puddings with various fillings top the popularity list. You can eat any day between 12 noon and 2 pm and, in the evening, between 7 pm and 9 pm. To quench your thirst, the Theakston range, Newcastle Exhibition, weekly guest beers and draught Woodpecker cider are ever on tap. Good wines are always available (bad whines unknown). Children are welcome, but not dogs – except guide dogs, of course.

Telephone: 01388 528160.

How to get there: Stanhope is on the A689, some 5½ miles west of Wolsingham. The Queen's Head is on the right-hand side of the road, 200 yards east of the market place.

Parking: None is available at the pub, but there are car parks in the market place, 200 yards to the west, and in the Durham Dales Centre.

Length of the walk: 4½ miles. OS map: Outdoor Leisure 31 Teesdale (inn GR 998391).

The well-signposted Weardale Way provides a clear trail to the walk's apex, at which elevated point the true extent of the mining and quarrying that took place around Stanhope can be seen and the relationship between industry and agriculture put into perspective. A fascinating and airy excursion into yesteryear.

The Walk

From the Queen's Head turn right along Stanhope's main street as far as the market place, which fronts the church of St Thomas the Apostle. The present building stands on the site of an earlier, wooden, one. It has had its share of eminent rectors, no less than eight of whom have become

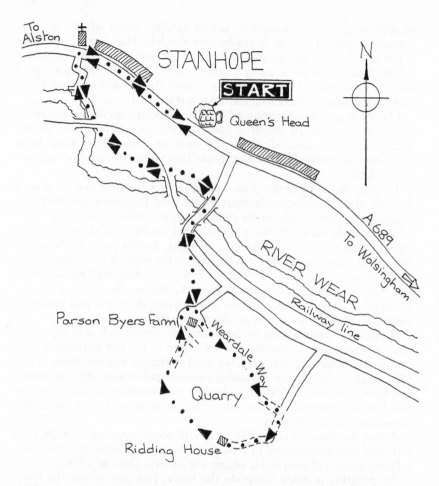

bishops, and has been called 'one of the most perfect and interesting of the ecclesiastical structures of the Middle Ages in the country'.

Turn left along a descending road that curves right. When almost at the end, turn left along a lane which backs the gardens of cottages on the left and soon edges the river on the right. At its end, cross the railway line where it spans the river Wear and continue across the middle of the field ahead, following the Weardale Way. Edge the next field and bear right over the third, a playing field, to regain the river, which you edge for a short distance. On reaching the railway, again where it bridges the river, cross the line and continue close to the river on your right, leaving the field over a facing, waymarked stile.

Turn right along a minor road that soon bridges the river and climbs steeply to go over the railway before turning sharp left. In a short distance a row of houses is reached on the left. Here turn right, over a waymarked stile and go diagonally left, up the facing field, following a line of telegraph poles along a green track. Leave the field through a stile on your left and pass in front of Parson Byers Farm on your right, continuing along a short lane and a farm track.

On reaching a post carrying a Weardale Way sign go diagonally right, uphill, as directed. As height is gained, a stile comes into view on the left. Cross it and descend, diagonally right, to cross narrow Cow Burn at another Weardale Way marker post. There is no bridge, the beck has little width.

Keeping in the same direction, continue over the field and leave over a facing stile. Go diagonally right to the field boundary and turn left, alongside it, until a stile on the right is reached, which you cross.

Immediately turn left, along a field track to its end, where you turn right, uphill, soon to pass a ruin on the right. At this point the Weardale Way goes left, over a stile, but you stay on the track, which soon curves right, climbing steadily, then bears left to reach Ridding House. Go to the right of it and cross a rough pasture, still on the track. Continue through a facing, left-hand corner gate, leaving the track, and gradually edge towards the rim of a huge, disused quarry on the right.

Weardale's contribution to the Industrial Revolution was supplying lead ore, iron ore, whinstone and limestone to the fast developing new industries. Sandstone was used for local buildings and dry-stone walls. When cheaper lead became available from abroad around 1890, the mines slid into recession. Today the lead mines and workings and the iron ore and limestone quarries are now reverting to nature and are a fascinating reminder of a very busy past.

Where the fence on your right turns left, across your line of walk, turn left, as it does and descend to cross Cow Burn. Climb the far bank, cross a facing fence and turn right, edging the quarry, close to a fence.

As progress is made alongside the fence, just past where the fence protrudes like a finger, a track is joined. Go along it, at first close to the quarry, but later, where the fence ends, pulling away from it, diagonally left, towards an impressive bank of conifers.

As the ground begins to fall away before you, excellent views are exposed. Then the track descends to a crossing of tracks, where you keep straight ahead, descending behind Parson Byers Farm and curving right to regain the outward route at the stile at the top of the field with the line of telegraph posts.

Because there is only one road bridge over the Wear hereabouts, retrace your steps from here, back to Stanhope and the Queen's Head.

15 Ireshopeburn
The Ranch

In its upper reaches the river Wear provides some of the most picturesque country in the county. Divers streams tumble from moorclad heights, gathering to become the Wear, which belongs entirely to County Durham. It flows along a narrow, green valley hemmed in by lofty fells. The A689 has to climb to a height of 2,056 ft above sea level to leave Weardale and one of the highest villages through which it passes is Ireshopeburn, a neat settlement of robust dwellings.

In 1854 a school was built at the hamlet's eastern approaches. Closed in 1909, it became a guest house and in 1971 was converted into the Rancho Del Rio, the name shortened today to the Ranch. One of its dining rooms is set out like the interior of a covered wagon, by use of canvas covers and with wall murals at each end depicting Wild West desert scenes. This gives the effect of being inside a 'prairie schooner'. Original, very clever and oh, so effective! A good range of fine fare is on offer at the pub, from a sandwich to a steak. The menus, we are told, are suggestions to be altered to suit individual requirements and vegetarian meals and special dietary needs are catered for. Morning coffee, afternoon and high teas are daily events, and main meals are as varied as roast turkey, steak and kidney pie, and chicken chasseur.

Sweets include a choice of gateaux, sherry trifle and fresh fruit salad. A sample Sunday lunch is roast beef and Yorkshire pudding, roast and boiled potatoes and vegetables of the day. Food is generally served from 12 noon to 2 pm and 7 pm to 9.30 pm every day. As for drinks, Stones, Bass and guest ales, house, French and German wines are all available. The Ranch has a 'no smoking' area, a family room, an exceptionally beautiful riverside beer garden and a play area for children. It is a freehouse, residential, and well-behaved dogs are welcome.

Telephone: 01388 537391.

How to get there: Take the A689 westwards up Weardale and a mile beyond St John's Chapel, on approaching Ireshopeburn, the Ranch is on the right.

Parking: There is ample parking in the grounds of the Ranch.

Length of the walk: 3 miles. OS map: Outdoor Leisure 31 Teesdale (inn GR 874384).

Here the Wear is frolicsome, spilling over small falls in its youthful enthusiasm to rendezvous with the distant sea. An excellent riverside path enables you to share its eagerness. A steepish climb up the valley side is compensated for by an equally steep descent, both allowing unparalleled views of the head of this lovely, lonely vale. Down the centuries Weardale farmers and their livestock have improved the poor soils and grasses to the sweet meadows of today. This circular walk will enable you to judge how efficiently the dale's head farmers have fulfilled this task. You will be pleasantly surprised. Spare time, too, to visit the splendid Weardale Museum, back in Ireshopeburn.

The Walk
From the Ranch turn right, along the A689, for a few yards and on reaching the Weardale Museum of High House Chapel, continue round the back of the building to avoid a rather dangerous kink in the road.

This fascinating place concentrates on life in Weardale towards the end of Queen Victoria's reign. It contains a typical living room of 100 years ago, where most of the domestic work was done. Five essential pieces of equipment are shown there – the cast iron fire range, a scrubbed, deal table, a large bowl, miscellaneous buckets and a small, galvanised bath. The single room upstairs is named after John Wesley, who visited Weardale in the 18th century. The adjoining chapel, still used as a place of worship, contains an organ dating from 1872. There is a fine collection of local minerals, donated by a local man. A fossil collection is being built up.

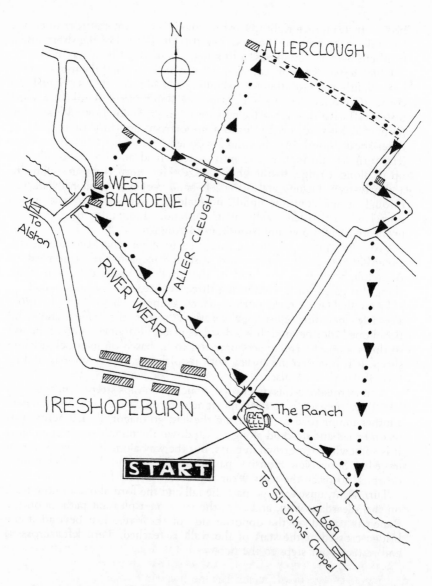

Go past the museum for a few yards and turn right, crossing the Wear on a bridge, to join the Weardale Way. Turn left along a riverside path, upstream, soon to go under a bridge that leads to a mine on your right. Continue, now on a track, for a further ½ mile to reach West Blackdene, where a bridge carrying a minor road spans the river. Do not cross this bridge. Instead, turn right towards the hamlet and where the road curves left, turn right, between houses. Towards the far end of the short street, turn left, between buildings, into a field, as directed by a waymarker.

Climb a steep bank ahead, using a flight of steps, from the top of which bear slightly right, up the field, climbing steadily to exit at its right-hand corner. Continue diagonally right up the sloping field ahead for a short distance. Leave through a facing gate to the right of Low Whitestones Farm. Go forward, briefly, onto a minor road and turn right along it. After about ¼ mile, just beyond a wooded ghyll, Aller Cleugh, on your left, turn left through a gate into a steep field and go diagonally left up it, along a ridge, to the ghyll's edge. Here turn right and climb to a clearly-seen, facing gate in the left-hand corner of a facing wall. Go through it and continue uphill, now along a very narrow field which funnels almost to lane width at its top end. Mountain pansies grow in profusion here, flowering from May to August.

Cross two pieces of rusting gate, tied together, and keep ahead, still alongside the ghyll, for a short distance to join the farm road to Allerclough Farm at the head of the ghyll on your left. Turn right, along this gated track, contouring three fields to reach a minor road.

From the farm track glorious views embrace the whole of Upper Teesdale including Burnhope reservoir across the valley and wild Burnhope Moor beyond. It is a desolate place, ill-drained, with acidic soil so thin the local farming economy has to be based on livestock, mainly sheep. It is home to the curlew with its plaintive, liquid 'coor-li' and its love of damp, open places.

Turn right, along this quiet road, which soon dips steeply and zig-zags left, then right. Where it turns right a second time at a point where another minor road meets it from the left, go diagonally left across this second road and descend along a path down the middle of a walled lane. It is somewhat overgrown in parts, but the way along it is never severely impeded. Soon New House is passed on the left and the path continues downhill to reach the river Wear just below a waterfall.

Turn right, upstream, go past the fall and the ford above it, now back on the Weardale Way, and edge the river on a pleasant path. Soon the Ranch is passed on the opposite side of the river. Just beyond it the bridge crossed at the start of the walk is reached. Turn left, across it, and retrace your steps to the pub.

16 Durham City
The Royal County Hotel

Durham is one of the most visually exciting cities in Britain. The Norman cathedral and the castle which form its centrepiece stand proudly on a sandstone bluff at a steep, wooded bend of the Wear, which almost encloses it like a moat.

The Royal County Hotel is sited close to the outer bank of the Wear as it curls around the bluff, east of the castle, near Elvet Bridge. It was formerly two houses built in 1630. Lady Mary Radcliffe, whose half sister, Lady Mary Tudor, was the natural daughter of Charles II, lived in one; Elizabeth Bowes, aunt of Lord Strathmore's wife, Mary Eleanor Bowes, lived in the other. In compliance with her father's will, when Mary married, her husband was to take her family name, so John Lyon, Earl of Strathmore, assumed the name of Bowes. From the joining of these families was to come our present Queen Mother. In the mid-19th century the houses were incorporated into a hotel, originally called the Dunelm. There is a carved, black oak staircase in the hotel that is even older than the original building. It was salvaged from ruined Loch Leven Castle in Scotland, where Mary Queen of Scots was a prisoner.

Even before it became a hotel famous personages stayed there. Cromwell did in 1650, on the way to the battle of Dunbar. Charles I hid there before his arrest for treason. More recently, Edward VII was a guest and it was then that the dignity of 'Royal' was added to the 'County'. Annually, on the third Saturday of July, until recently when most of Durham's coalfields were closed, leading Labour politicians would appear on the hotel balcony to view the proceedings at the Durham Miners' Gala.

As the hotel has expanded every effort has been made to ensure that the old and the new have blended comfortably. It is opulent and smoothly efficient but exudes bonhomie. In the County Restaurant, where the elite meet to eat, an exceptionally high quality menu includes such gastronomic delights as saddle of lamb, sliced onto a potato rosti covered in a rich rosemary juice. This restaurant serves lunch daily between 12 noon and 2.30 pm and dinner from 7.30 pm to 10.15 pm (9.30 pm on Sunday). The Brasserie, open all day, has a wide range of hot and cold food for lunch and dinner and its chef will happily advise on the day's display. Vegetarian dishes include quorn tikka masala with saffron rice. Chicken and bacon club sandwiches with salad garnish and French fries could be among the specials. The bar is decorated on the theme of the Durham Light Infantry. Vaux-linked, it offers a hand-pulled Wards Best Bitter while Lorimer's Scotch and Samson beers and Labatt's and Heineken lagers are on draught.

Telephone: 0191 3866821.

How to get there: Approaching Durham from the south, along the A167, turn right at the Cock O'the North, along the A1050. On reaching a roundabout keep straight ahead along Church Street, which meets New Elvet at a tangent. Continue along it to where Old Elvet is crossed. The Royal County Hotel is on the far right-hand corner.

Parking: There is a very large car park at the rear of the hotel, entered through an archway.

Length of the walk: 2½ miles. OS map: Pathfinder 572 (inn GR 277424).

The twin towers of Durham Cathedral are breathtaking, particularly when viewed from a train approaching from the south. Both cathedral and castle head an exceptional list of sites and buildings noted for their splendour and involvement with English history that are seen on this fascinating journey into our glorious past.

The Walk

From the hotel entrance in old Elvet turn right and cross New Elvet. Cross Elvet Bridge, the original of which was built by Bishop Puiset

The Last Supper – wood carvings seen on the route near Prebend's Bridge.

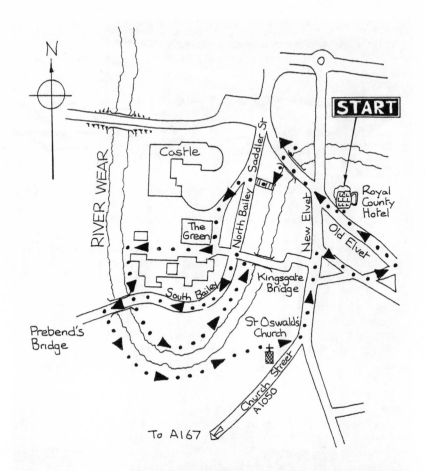

(1153–95), and immediately turn right, descend steps and turn right again along the riverside path. Go under the bridge and along Fearon Walk for 100 yards. Turn right, up a stepped vennel, Drury Lane, the site of an 18th-century theatre.

From its top turn left, along Saddler Street, then first right, briefly, along Owngate with its 15th-century Tudor house, to the Palace Green.

The Palace Green, formerly 'The Place', lies between the cathedral and the castle, which was also the bishops' palace. When the castle was handed over to the university the bishops used Auckland Castle as their only residence.

Edge to its left-hand side, passing 18th-century Abbey House, an almshouse dated 1668, and Bishop Cosin's Hall, a magnificent 17th-century mansion. Turn right alongside the cathedral, where a short detour left, through the door with the splendid sanctuary knocker, leads into the greatest Norman church in England.

Begun in 1093, it was completed in 1133. The Galilee Chapel (c 1170), the Chapel of Nine Altars (c 1242) and the central tower (c 1490) are later additions.

Once past the cathedral continue between buildings along Windy Gap. At a junction of paths turn left for 25 yards, then go right, down a zig-zag path and past a well, to the riverside. Turn left along a riverside path, passing the old fulling mill, now the Museum of Archaeology, and the weir. Stay on the path, passing Prebend's Bridge, and continue edging the river.

In a short distance Colin Wilbourne's exceptional work, carved from elms and called 'The Upper Room', is passed, beyond which a small folly is reached. It stands near where the Polish dwarf Count Borowlaski lived.

On reaching Kingsgate Bridge turn left, up steps and, at the top, turn left, along Bow Lane, passing, on the right, St Mary-le-Bow, the possible site of the White Church where the body of St Cuthbert rested during the building of the cathedral.

Turn left along North Bailey, passing the 13th-century Chapel of the Nine Altars on the right.

Pass the gateway to the College Green, with its early Georgian architecture. North Bailey becomes South Bailey, with its grand doorways, and, continuing, you go through Watergate Arch, erected in 1778.

Here bear left to cross Prebend's Bridge, rebuilt in 1772 to replace the original, which was destroyed by flood in 1771.

Turn left along a riverside path until just past where a watercourse is crossed on a culvert, where you turn right, along a narrow, stepped path, which soon contours. At its end turn left, briefly, then right, along another path. Soon St Oswald's church is passed on the right.

St Oswald, King of Northumbria, became a Christian in Iona, and invited St Aidan to settle on Lindisfarne to convert his kingdom to Christianity. He died fighting Penda, pagan King of Mercia, in AD 642. His severed head is in St Cuthbert's tomb.

Just past the church the path curves right, through the churchyard, beyond which you bear left along a footpath, crossing the road to a right-hand one when traffic allows. Continue downhill and just past Barclay's Bank turn right along Elvet Crescent. Continue along Court Lane, which soon turns sharp left. The road then curves right, then left, to join Old Elvet. Turn left along it, soon to pass the old Shire Hall, beyond where, on the right, is the Royal County Hotel.

17 Lanchester
The King's Head

Lanchester is named after the Roman fort of Longovicium, situated on a hill ¹/₂ mile south-west of the village. It was built in AD 122 to guard part of Dere Street, which linked York to Hadrian's Wall.

All Saints' church, with its four-square, battlemented tower, dominates the village. Opposite it, a wide, tree-bedecked green is flanked by prosperous-looking stone houses, shops and the very pleasant King's Head, a Scottish and Newcastle house, where Exhibition, McEwan's Scotch and lager, Theakston traditional ale and Matthew Brown Bitter are on offer. Inside, the well-appointed bar shares the same large room as the dining area – an arrangement that works well. The menu, which changes constantly, is as long as your arm, and the day's fare is displayed on notice boards at the front of the pub. Vegetarians are well catered for, and The King's Platter which includes steak, gammon, liver, black pudding, tomatoes, onion rings, fried egg and french fried potatoes, is a favourite on the à la carte menu. Bar food is available throughout opening times, except on Saturday evenings and Sunday lunchtimes, when the restaurant menu applies. Outside, there is a beer garden and a children's play area. Dogs are welcome.

Telephone: 01207 520054.

How to get there: Lanchester is 7 miles north-west of Durham City along the A691, where four major roads meet. Where, in the village, the B6296 branches left, just west of All Saints' church, the King's Head is on the left, facing the green.

Parking: You can park at the rear of the pub.

Length of the walk: 4 miles. OS map: Pathfinder 571 (inn GR 167474).

Lanchester is surrounded by good, hilly, well-wooded countryside, which this easily-tackled, mainly field walk explores. For the final mile the route follows the Lanchester Valley Walk, a disused railway now a haven for interesting plants and wildlife.

The Walk
From the King's Head cross the road and continue across the village green, bearing slightly right to the A691, which you go over at a crossing. Turn left along a roadside footpath for about 50 yards to turn right at a footpath sign. Go along a short tarmac lane, using a wayside footpath. At the lane end cross a wall stile on your left and turn right along a clear path, edging a field. Exit over a stile in the right-hand corner of a facing hedge. Go straight up the next field close to its right-hand side, following a climbing path that curves left, then right, between shrubs, to reach a stile in the right-hand corner of a facing hedge, which you cross. Continue straight ahead, close to a ditch and hedge on the right, then alongside a mix of hedge and fence.

From here the retrospective view of Lanchester, in the valley bottom, is very good indeed.

On reaching a facing fence, turn left alongside it for about 30 yards, then go through a gateway in a step in the fence. Once through it, go diagonally right, up the hillside, going through a gap in the gorse bushes to a clearly-seen stile in the fence on your right, met at a tangent. Cross it and go straight ahead, close to a wall on your right, now on level ground, towards Moor Leazes Farm, seen ahead.

Where the wall on the right ends, just short of the farm, turn right, along a track that edges the field ahead.

The countryside hereabouts is most attractive. It is a series of lateral ridges spreading eastwards from the Pennines. The views are very good indeed.

Once across the field, the track goes through a facing gateway and immediately turns right, close to a wall on the right. Do likewise and on reaching the end of this field, leave the track short of a gap, turn left and edge the field close to a hedge on your right. It is a long field and you leave it over a facing right-hand corner stile onto the B6296.

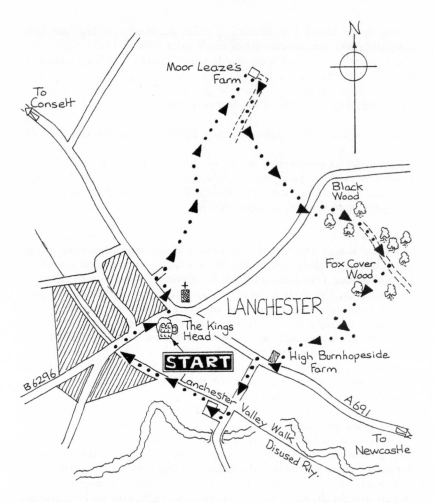

Immediately turn right for only 7 yards, keeping close to the road's edge, because of the bend in it. As soon as a footpath sign is seen on the opposite side, cross the road with care. Go over a stile in a step in the hedge and follow a clear woodland path, descending to cross a stream on a plank bridge and climbing out of the wood through a waymarked stile.

Continue along a very clear path, diagonally left, climbing across rough pasture, to enter Black Wood and go straight through it. Here the wood is thin and, once through it, the path continues in the same direction between a mix of freshly planted conifers and deciduous trees to Foxcover Wood, seen ahead.

Enter the woodland over a stile and follow a most pleasant, contouring ride, with Lanchester valley below on your right. Soon a path leads off to the right. Take it and in a few yards, where it splits, take the right fork, descending, at first through woodland, continuing just inside it, close to a fence on the right. Soon the path turns left, still inside the wood. In about 25 yards, just before some Scots pines, turn right over a stile into a field. Cross it diagonally right, descending. Exit through a gate beneath a large sycamore tree in the field's corner. Turn left, edging the next field and just short of High Burnhopeside Farm, seen ahead, turn left, over a stile. Go forward for about 25 yards and, when the fence on the right ends, turn right to the A691.

Turn right, along a roadside footpath, soon to reach a signpost to Malton, where you turn left, over the main road, taking care, and continue along a minor one, met end on.

Take the first turning right, through the car park of Malton picnic area. Continue across the picnic area itself to join the Lanchester Valley Walk along a disused railway track, met at a tangent.

Now simply continue along the old trackbed for about a mile to where the B6296 crosses it. Here leave the trackbed, right, going along a street towards the village green, where the King's Head awaits.

Beamish
The Shepherd and Shepherdess

Beamish Open Air Museum is world renowned and brings many visitors to this rural hamlet in the far north of the county.

The Shepherd and Shepherdess is to be found at a road junction to the south of the museum. Columns at the pub's main entrance support a lintel on which two figures, a shepherd and shepherdess, of course, stand in eye-catching splendour. The statues were originally endowed with the ability to become mortal during the hours of darkness and would dance the night away with the fairies. One night, they almost left it too late to return to their pedestals, and in their confusion leaped onto the wrong ones. There they remain to this day, he on hers, she on his.

The pub they adorn is a listed building of great charm, bedecked in summer with glorious hanging baskets, balls of living colour. The interior is cosy and welcoming, with an open fire on colder days. Lunches are served on Monday to Saturday from 12 noon to 2 pm, and on Sunday from 11.30 am to 2.30 pm. Evening meals are from 7 pm to 9.30 pm (10 pm on Saturday). There is a choice of starters and the main course ranges from mince and leek pudding through poached salmon with crab sauce to a choice of steaks, rump, sirloin or T-bone, vegetarian lasagne or quiche. The pub is a Vaux house, selling Wards

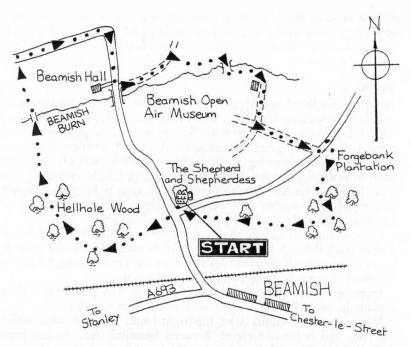

Bitter, Samson and Waggle Dance, Lorimer's Scotch and Beamish stout. Ciders on draught are Woodpecker and Strongbow. The extensive wine list includes reds and whites from Australia, Bulgaria, California, Chile, France, Germany and Italy. There is outside seating, close to a wooded play area complete with a slide. Children are welcome in the family room – but, sorry, no dogs.

Telephone: 0191 3700349.

How to get there: Take the A693 westwards from Chester-le-Street via Pelton. After 5 miles turn right just past Beamish village, and after ¼ mile arrive at the Shepherd and Shepherdess, on the right.

Parking: There is ample space in the pub car park alongside the building.

Length of the walk: 4 miles. OS map: Pathfinder 562 (inn GR 221538).

At Beamish Open Air Museum you can step back in time and see the North-East of yesteryear as it was. Old homes have been reconstructed, brick by brick – and the site's old shops, the drift mine, fun fair, farm and working railway have won acclaim. A Gateshead No 10 tramcar travels a route close to this fascinating walk, which is ever near the museum's boundary. Woodland paths, pleasant tracks and a little road walking make this circuit a treat; and there are some close views of Beamish Hall for good measure.

The Walk

From the Shepherd and Shepherdess cross the road and go through a metal gap stile alongside a gate, into woodland. Follow a clear path and when it bifurcates go left, into Eden Place picnic area car park, which you cross. Continue along a tarmac track, briefly, to a T-junction, where you turn right, passing another parking area on the left. Stay on this track, soon to reach another junction, where you turn left, leaving the picnic area. In a few yards, where the track splits, turn right, past a barrier, into woodland, soon to edge another parking area. Continue from its left-hand corner along a lane, guided by a yellow arrow.

On reaching a facing gate go through a gap stile alongside it and follow a clear track through Hellhole Wood. At its end, where paths split, go left, along a path which almost at once bears right to go through a facing, waymarked gap stile, and continue along the path.

From here many of the varied trees by the path have plaques near them explaining, very cleverly in verse, each one's characteristics.

Where the path splits take the right-hand, broader, one, which descends and becomes stepped, between beautiful trees, to exit from the wood into Beamish Burn picnic area. In a few yards the path curves right to edge Beamish Burn briefly, then cross it on a footbridge into the picnic area car park.

Beamish Hall kitchen garden wall, on the right, is rare because it is hollow and was once used to protect the fruit trees from frost by being heated.

Continue through the picnic area on a surfaced track and turn right along a minor road, between great splashes of blues and purples when the rhododendrons are out. In about $1/2$ mile the road makes a right-angled turn, so take care. Stay on it, descending, and turn left along a clear streamside track when opposite the entrance to Beamish Hall, which was acquired for the museum in 1970.

Beamish Open Air Museum, where the olden days are brought so brilliantly to life, is just across the stream.

Follow the track to where three concrete boulders are laid across it and turn right, along a descending lane. Exit over a waymarked stile and continue along a green path towards the stream ahead, where you turn left along an edging path. Cross a facing stile and continue downstream. On reaching a facing fence cross a stile in the fence on your left. Immediately turn right, continuing down the meandering stream on a clear path, passing waymarkers. Cross a facing stile, go forward for a few yards and turn right, over the stream, on a concrete bridge. Follow a clear, uphill track for some 40 yards and turn left over a waymarked stile. Continue along a clear path, which soon climbs a bank to a facing stile near a waymarker on a post. Cross the stile into a field, turn left, briefly, to a gate in the fence on your left, which you go through. Now follow a clear path along a wooded bank high above the stream on your left. Cross a facing stile and take a short, field track that curves left, descending towards a building. Just before it turn right, along a climbing path, to cross a facing stile.

Pass a farmhouse on the right and keep straight ahead along a farm track. At a crossing of tracks turn left, climbing steeply.

From this track the surrounding rolling, well-wooded countryside is seen to advantage.

On reaching a minor road turn left along it, downhill, and where the road curves left, turn right at a footpath sign, into Forgebank Plantation. Follow a clear path which soon climbs steeply. On reaching a path at right angles, go right, along it. Where it splits go left, directed by a yellow arrow. Soon this path climbs and curves left. When it splits take the right-hand fork. On meeting another facing track turn right along it, leaving the plantation, onto a road. Bear left along it, briefly, back to the pub on the right-hand side – and the misplaced shepherd and shepherdess.

Note: During the summer months Beamish Museum is open every day. During the winter it concentrates on the town area only, and is closed on Monday and Friday. The opening hours throughout the year are from 10 am to 5 pm, last admission being 3 pm. The museum's entrance is just along the road from the pub.

Causey Arch
The Causey Arch Inn

From the elevated lounge windows of the pub there is a splendid view of the surrounding countryside, including a wooded gorge which is spectacular enough in its own right, even without its splendid centrepiece, Causey Arch, the oldest railway bridge of its kind in the world.

In the upstairs restaurant of this traditional family pub, where good food is offered in a friendly, cosy atmosphere, the set menu is augmented by the chef's specials, displayed on a blackboard. His home-made curries and sauté beef in red wine and tomato sauce are extra good. Soup of the day is always home-made, fish dishes include deep fried plaice Dieppe and main courses like Westmorland pie are a temptation. For snacks there are baked potatoes with a choice of fillings and freshly made sandwiches. There is also a menu for children. Lunch is served between 12 noon and 2 pm every day, and evening meals are between 7 pm and 10 pm. There is no food on Sunday evenings. This is a freehouse, with Theakston Best Bitter and Old Peculier very popular in 'the 19th hole'. Woodpecker and Scrumpy Jack ciders and red and white wines are also on offer. There is a seating area outside and well-behaved dogs are welcome, there and in the bar. Overnight accommodation is available.

Telephone: 01207 233925.

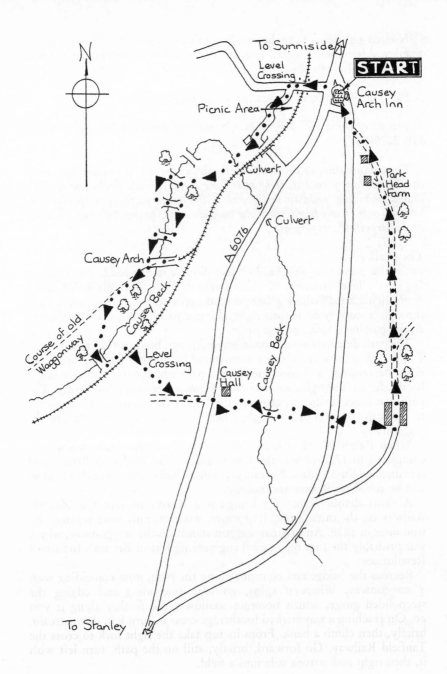

To Sunniside

Level Crossing

START

Causey Arch Inn

Picnic Area

Park Head Farm

Culvert

Culvert

A6076

Causey Arch

Causey Beck

Course of old Waggonway

Level Crossing

Causey Beck

Causey Hall

To Stanley

How to get there: Take the A6076 southwards from Sunniside towards Stanley. After some 2 miles, you will find the pub occupying an elevated position on the left side of the road.

Parking: There is a large car park fronting the pub.

Length of the walk: 3½ miles. OS maps: Pathfinder 561 and 562 (inn GR 207563).

The combination of the Tanfield Railway, the world's oldest line, built in 1725 to carry coal to the river Tyne, and Causey Arch, the world's oldest surviving railway bridge, now the centrepiece of a spectacular, silvan gorge, itself laced with old waggonways, makes this superb walk an unforgettable experience.

The Walk

From the pub cross the A6076 and follow a minor road, met end on. Go over a level crossing, 50 yards beyond which turn left into Causey Arch picnic area. Follow a tarmac road across it and just before it exits through a railway arch turn right along a path signposted 'to Causey Arch', passing a toilet on the right.

The path descends a man-made embankment, built in 1725 to carry the Tanfield Waggonway, which was powered by horses. Where it splits, go right, descending, and continue along a path which curves left, passing a footbridge on the right, soon to cross Causey Beck on a footbridge. The path continues upstream, crossing the burn twice more on footbridges, to reach the bottom of the Arch, where you turn right, up steps, to the waggonway.

When Ralph Wood, a local stonemason, built the Arch, which was completed in 1727, it was the largest single-span bridge in Britain and remained so for 30 years. No one previously had ever built such a bridge, and he relied on Roman technology.

A short detour across the bridge is a 'must', to visit the Tanfield Railway on the other bank. Its former, wooden, rails were replaced by iron ones in 1839. An original waggon stands on the waggonway, which was probably the first major civil engineering feat of Britain's Industrial Revolution.

Recross the bridge and continue along the path, now coinciding with a waggonway. Where it splits, go left, descending and edging the steep-sided gorge, which becomes shallower the further along it you go. On reaching a waymarked footbridge cross it, turn left, downstream, briefly, then climb a bank. From its top take the right fork to cross the Tanfield Railway. Go forward, briefly, still on the path, turn left with it, then right and cross a stile into a field.

Go along the field's left side, uphill, leave through a facing, waymarked gateway and descend to a facing track. Turn left along it to the A6076, which you cross. Descend steps at a footpath sign and at the embankment's foot turn right, as waymarked. In 25 yards turn left over a stile into a field. Follow a green path, edging a hedge on your left with Causey Hall beyond it. Exit over a facing stile in the field's left-hand corner. Continue diagonally left, guided by a yellow arrow, and on reaching the corner of the Hall's garden, turn right, along a clear, descending path, close to the fence on the right. Near the right-hand corner leave the field down steps.

From the bottom step the path goes diagonally right across a narrow field to go over Causey Beck on a waymarked footbridge. The path now bears right, then left, to a clearly-seen facing, waymarked step stile. Cross it, climb a steep bank on steps and from the top continue, edging the field's right-hand boundary. Exit over a facing stile in its right-hand corner onto a minor road.

Turn right along it for 50 yards, then turn left, towards a gateway, but do not go through it. Instead, turn left again, guided by a footpath sign, and go through a gap stile into a wooded area. Follow a path, diagonally right, through it. Exit over a facing stile at its right-hand corner. Immediately turn right and right again, through a gate. Turn left, edge the field ahead, leaving through a waymarked gap stile at the left-hand corner of a facing fence. Go diagonally right across the field ahead, leaving through a facing stile in its right-hand corner. Edge the next field close to a right-hand fence. Exit over a facing stile and continue along a short lane into Coppy.

Turn left along an unsurfaced road. Where it bifurcates and the right-hand fork goes through a metal gate, go left, through a small gate and along a clear track. Where it curves left into Park Head Farm, keep straight ahead on a clear path, soon to join a concrete track at a tangent. Continue along it, descending, to a minor road. Turn right along it, back to the Causey Arch Inn, seen ahead.

20 Ebchester
The Derwent Walk Inn

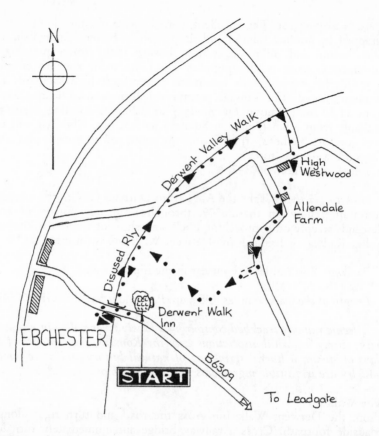

The Romans built a fort, Vindomora, where Dere Street crosses the river Derwent. Today it is the border village of Ebchester, and you can find here a small museum containing information about the fort. The B6309 climbs steeply south-easterly out of Ebchester and in less than ½ mile bridges the defunct Derwent Valley Railway. Here, adjacent to Ebchester station, the Station Hotel stood. It was destroyed in a fire which killed the landlord, rebuilt in 1947 and later renamed the Derwent Walk Inn after the walk the old line had become.

A refreshing drink or a delicious meal in this award-winning but traditional country pub, with unrivalled views over the Derwent Valley and Northumberland beyond, complements a memorable walk perfectly. The atmosphere is convivial, the staff friendly and unobtrusive, there is a roaring fire on cold days, a beer garden for warmer weather, and a splendid range of real ales, Tetley, Marston's Pedigree and Burton among them. Gaymer's and Bulmers original ciders are on draught and there is a wine list. The excellent, varied menu includes king prawns wrapped in smoked salmon and deep fried in batter, Cajun fish, and fillet, sirloin and rump steaks. For dessert, sticky toffee pudding in butterscotch sauce is very popular. The home-made rhubarb crumble is wonderful – and there's lots more of the same high standard. The children's menu offers sausage, scampi or half portions. Lunch is served from 11.30 am (12 noon on Sunday) to 2.30 pm. Evening meals are available from 6 pm (7 pm on Sunday) to 9.30 pm. Children will feel very comfortable here – there is a family room and an outside play area. Dogs are welcome, too.

Telephone: 01207 560347.

How to get there: Take the A691 from Durham City north-westerly, continuing, now on the B6309, through Leadgate. Where the road descends steeply on approaching Ebchester, short of where the Derwent Valley Railway is bridged, the Derwent Walk Inn is on the right.

Parking: You can leave your car in the inn's car park.

Length of the walk: 3 miles. OS map: Pathfinder 561 (inn GR 107547).

A scenic railway trackbed contouring a lovely river valley in a country park, strong historical associations with the Romans, the romance of the days of steam, a liberal sprinkling of natural history and a welcoming hostelry are irresistible ingredients in this most enjoyable walk.

The Walk

From the Derwent Walk Inn cross the road and turn right along a roadside footpath. Cross a railway bridge and immediately turn left, down some steps and along a short path to the disused Derwent Valley Railway.

The old line ran for 11 miles between Swalwell and Consett and in 1972 the Derwent Walk, along its trackbed, was opened. Its surface is suitable for cycles, horses and wheelchairs as well as for those on foot.

Turn left, along it, going under the bridge and past the site of Ebchester station, now a car park and picnic area. Continue along the trackbed, flat as a pancake hereabouts, as it goes along the top of a very high, arboreal embankment, beyond which it descends, then rises, where a bridge has been removed.

The Derwent Walk is the centrepiece of the Derwent Walk Country Park, one of the largest country parks in the north-east of England. The park, which never closes, has grown to contain woodlands, meadows, ponds and riverside areas that can be enjoyed by anyone with a love of the countryside.

Stay on the trackbed, soon to cross metalled Shaw Lane, continuing along the route of the old railway.

Below, to the left, the river Derwent flows; and, beyond it, is Northumberland.

The trackbed continues through a cutting where the woodland verges are lush and hold a wide variety of wildlife. Field scabious, rosebay willowherb and foxgloves grow among the silver birc!.es, sycamores, hazels and brambles in a glorious kaleidoscope, ever-changing in colour and form. It is an area frequented by the green and great spotted woodpecker, nuthatches and ubiquitous magpies, among many other birds. With luck, roe deer, foxes and even badgers may be glimpsed. These are shy creatures so quietness is of the essence.

Beyond the cutting a barrier is reached. Go through a gap at its side and descend a slope to where a lane crosses the trackbed at right angles. When the line was operating there was a bridge here.

Turn right, along the lane, steeply uphill, to the mining hamlet of High Westwood. When a facing minor road is met, cross it diagonally right and bear left at a footpath sign, passing the gable end of a row of dwellings on the right. Continue past the gable end along a short passage between gardens and over a stile into a field. Cross it diagonally right along a clear path, exiting at its far right-hand corner over a waymarked stile onto a road. Turn left, along it, uphill, passing Allandale Farm on the left.

As the road goes straight ahead before turning sharp right, reduce the angle by using a roadside footpath which, for a short distance, follows a more direct but steeper route to the hilltop. There used to be a village, Allandale Cottages, on top of this hill, but little remains.

Continue edging the hill's rim on a roadside footpath until a square, brick tower is passed. Just beyond it, turn right at a footpath sign and descend to go through a facing gate into a field. Go down a short, broad track to the foot of a slope and, where it ends, take the left-hand one of two paths, going diagonally left.

Where the path fades away, keep straight ahead to leave the field through a gateway in the right-hand corner of the fence on your left, met at a tangent. Immediately turn right, descending a rough pasture, close to a fence on the right. Just past a hawthorn and an elderberry close together, cross a stile in the fence. Follow the field path ahead, which bears left along Long Bank, keeping below the gorse bushes. The path becomes more defined the further you go along it. It cuts through a row of trees and continues diagonally left to the field corner, beyond which is the Derwent Valley Railway trackbed, walked on the outward leg. Exit from the field through a kissing-gate, turn left along the old line's route, and retrace your steps to the Derwent Walk Inn.